THE COMPUTER IN EDUCATION

A Critical Perspective

THE COMPUTER IN EDUCATION
A Critical Perspective

DOUGLAS SLOAN, Editor
Teachers College, Columbia University

Teachers College, Columbia University
New York and London

Published by Teachers College Press, 1234 Amsterdam Avenue, New York, N.Y. 10027

Grateful acknowledgment is made for permission to reprint Figures 1 through 4 on pages 13 and 14 from *Mindstorms: Children, Computers, and Powerful Ideas* by Seymour Papert. Copyright © 1980 by Basic Books, Inc. Reprinted by permission of the publisher. First published in Great Britain in 1980 by The Harvester Press, Ltd.

Library of Congress Cataloging in Publication Data

Main entry under title:

The Computer in education.

Includes bibliographies and index.
1. Education—Data processing. 2. Education—Aims and objectives. I. Sloan, Douglas.
LB1028.43.C638 1985 370'.28'5 85-4679

ISBN 0-8077-2782-2

Manufactured in the United States of America

90 89 88 87 86 85 1 2 3 4 5 6

Contents

Introduction: On Raising Critical Questions About the Computer in Education

DOUGLAS SLOAN
Teachers College, Columbia University

This collection of articles arises from a threefold conviction: that the computer offers potential for human betterment, and at the same time is fraught with great dangers to the human being; that neither the potential can be truly realized, nor the dangers avoided, without careful, far-reaching, critical questions being asked about the computer in education; and that American educators in general have been almost totally remiss in their responsibility to raise and pursue these critical questions.

Extolling the computer as a boon to critical thinking, professional educators by and large have been conspicuously uncritical about the computer itself. Scrambling to lead the van of the computer-communications revolution in education, American educators have made no concerted effort to ask at what level, for what purposes, and in what ways the computer is educationally appropriate and inappropriate, in what ways and to whom we can count on its being beneficial or harmful. The overall picture has been one, instead, of educators vying to outdo one another in thinking of new ways to use the computer in all manners and at every level of education possible. Professional responsibility demands more.

Why have American educators, apart from individual exceptions here and there,[1] so sedulously avoided the critical questions? Several possible answers come readily to mind. There are the obvious, not so flattering ones: Pushing computers is where the money is; it is better to be on the bandwagon than running to catch up, or standing in front of it; no one wants to be labeled a neo-Luddite, an anti-technologist, a nongrowth person, a matho-phobe and computer-anxious one, the kind of person who would also have opposed Gutenberg and Copernicus—all the epithets even the mildest computer critic often, indeed, finds himself saddled with.

But there are two deeper possible explanations for the lack of any concerted critical perspective on computers among modern educators. One is the widespread sense, expressed not only among educators, that the computer-communications revolution is inexorable, and that we have no choice but to accept and come to terms with it. Frequently the advent of the computer and its related electronic communications is compared to a third industrial revolution, which, like steam and electricity before it, can be expected to be all-pervasive in scale and scope, remorseless in its growth in that nothing can stop it, and unpredictable in its outcome in that no one knows what the long-range consequences will be. Chances are, this is all quite true. Hidden in this assumption, however, is often another, altogether different premise: namely, that human beings have no responsible choices whatsoever in shaping, restraining, and directing this revolution, that coming to terms with it means going along with it on its terms (and, what is not so often spoken aloud, on the terms of those who control and stand to profit from it). The responsible, mature person—the person who is not a crank or a hopeless romantic—will therefore, it is asserted, embrace the revolution, take it into his home, his children's classrooms, his own soul, enthusiastically, no questions asked. It is a strange notion of responsibility whose first and last act is self-abdication. We may be sure of one thing: If we ask no hard and critical questions, if we have learned nothing from the first two industrial revolutions that we can apply to the so-called third, if we give no thought and action to the consequences, the new technology (and the power of those who control it) will be totally irresistible and its effect irreversible.

There are those who assure us that misgivings and uneasiness are unfounded. They concede that the new technology may produce many casualties, but insist that these will be mainly among those who, not embracing the revolution, will be left in the dustbin of history. In most of its effects the revolution, we are assured, will be overwhelmingly benign. Among the anodynes proffered to calm any anxieties about technological progress, the analogy of the automobile is frequently cited. The computer, like the automobile, it is suggested, may entail some casualties but it will greatly enhance convenience, comfort, and the possibilities for personal communication among the majority of its users. One could feel much better about the example of the automobile if those who put it forward gave even the slightest indication that they are aware of the huge personal, social, and enviromental price that we have had, and have still, to pay for the convenience of its use.[2] Even if we accept without question the benign influence of the automobile for society at large as an apt metaphor for the benefits of the computer, there are still some all-important distinctions to be made. After all, we do not put our four-, five-, and six-year old children behind the wheel of the car; we do not do it for their sakes and for ours.

Unfortunately, there are many signs already that call for more than a technolatrous faith that the third revolution will inevitably turn out well in its social consequences. The growing real possibilities of using the computer for official, and not so official, surveillance and control of the citizenry is a direct threat to any concern for a democratic education.[3] The developing "industrial connection" between American education at all levels and computer, pharmaceutical, and defense industries mocks every notion of academic freedom.[4] It does not take a flaming Bolshevik, nor even a benighted neo-Luddite, to wonder whether all those computer companies, and their related textbook publishers, that are mounting media campaigns for computer literacy and supplying hundreds of thousands of computers to schools and colleges really have the interests of children and young people as their primary concern. The warning signs of increasing social, economic, and cultural inequalities and disruptions arising from the growth of high technology call for the best critical thought from those concerned with the career and vocational dimensions of education.[5] Educators have not even begun to face and grapple with the fact that the majority of graduates from university artifical intelligence programs will find, as Joseph Weizenbaum, computer scientist at M.I.T., has pointed out, that most of the jobs for them will be with companies working for the military.[6] All these questions deserve the most careful attention of educators who are at all concerned with the social consequences of their work.

But there are still much deeper, more fundamental issues to be raised and explored. And here we see yet another possible reason for the failure of a critical educational perspective on computers to develop. There is very little in the literature on computers to indicate any widespread sense of conflict between the dominantly accepted goals of modern education and the use of the computer. Increasingly, there appears a growing convergence of outlook among educators and the public that the chief goal of education is to develop the concrete-operational skills of technical reason coupled with functional, utilitarian language skills. That cognition involves a rationality much deeper and more capacious than technical reason is forgotten; that even the development of strong logic and technical reason itself may not best be served by the hot-house forcing of analytical and abstract thinking at an ever earlier age is overlooked.

In this context the computer is seen to recommend itself as the further extension and embodiment of these same goals and the preeminent means to their achievement. To question the computer in a rigorous way means, therefore, to begin also to ask critical questions about the whole of modern education as it has increasingly taken form even before and up to the advent of the computer. And this, one suspects, most modern educators are not so much unwilling as unable, because unprepared, to do. Moreover, at a time when the nation's schools are widely perceived to be in serious trouble, the computer seems for many people to have come on the scene as a veritable *deus ex machina* to put all things right, and to relieve parents, teachers, and all our sundry officials of any necessity for fundamental reexamination of self and society.

In the present climate, therefore, to call for a critical look at the computer in education will immediately be seen by many as by definition anticomputer and antitechnology and antitechnical reasoning. But to react in this way is to miss what is really at issue. The central question is not whether one is for or against computers in education, but to define the human and educational criteria and priorities that can make a truly human use of the computer possible. Such a critical look will be the first step in beginning to make much-needed distinctions and discriminations between what is appropriate and what is inappropriate, between what is helpful and what is damaging, in the uses and places of the computer for different purposes and for different types and ages of students. That which is appropriate, for example, for high school students and adults may be inappropriate and outright harmful for small and school-age children. It would not be the least benefit of such a critical inquiry if it were to enable people to thus begin to discriminate rigorously between the appropriate and the inappropriate, between the good and the hurtful, in the educational use of computers, without feeling, or being made to feel, that they had thereby to take a stand for or against computers as such. But to ask really penetrating questions about the place of the computer in education will not be easy, for it might well lead in directions and into areas of concern long neglected in American education.

One of these all-important educational concerns has to do with what the Scottish philosopher John Macmurray has called *emotional rationality*. Macmurray employs this expression to denote the central part played by the emotional-feeling life in cognition.[7] The main cognitive activity of the emotions is twofold. The emotions guide and empower logical reason, setting its goals and providing its energy. And, more important, feelings themselves, when properly developed and educated, work as our most penetrating and indispensable organs of cognition. It is only through a deep, feeling-awareness that we can come to know the qualitative dimension of life—in nature, in other persons, in ourselves. It is in this larger matrix of qualitative reality that all reason, including the logical and calculative, ultimately finds its ground. Macmurray stresses, therefore, that it is crucial to grasp the primacy of feeling in all cognition. He writes: "It is not that our feelings have a secondary and subordinate capacity for being rational or irrational. It is that reason is primarily an affair of emotion, and that the rationality of thought is the derivative and secondary one."[8] Qualitative knowing—the only kind capable of grasping living and personal reality—requires a rich, vital emotional life.

Merely having feelings, however, is not enough (some "get-'em-all-out" schools of popular therapy to the contrary notwithstanding). Just as we can have false reasons, we can have false emotions. For the feelings to serve as organs of cognition requires that they be nourished and educated—inner discipline, energetic attentiveness, and discrimination are essential.

Modern education often seems, however, to have lost all sense of the cognitive significance of the feeling-emotional life. To be sure, a few educational psychologists champion the importance of "affective education," but almost always set it off against "cognitive education," and as a result probably do more harm than good. Otherwise, in most modern educational settings the feelings seem to be regarded mainly as problems—if they cannot be held in check, perhaps they can be channeled off, as in athletics—or are seen as opportunities for exploitation—"capture their interest," "make learning fun."[9] By relegating feeling to the realm of the peripheral in education, we not only weaken and short-circuit thinking, we leave individuals and society aswim in feelings that are unformed, maudlin, and brutish. A people whose feeling sensibilities are more and more dulled and coarsened will quickly lose the capacity to recognize that the health of society can never be gained through the gross national product, a new election, technological advance, bigger defense spending. The atrophy of feeling-perception will have cut this people off from communion with the essential qualities of life.

What then does an education of emotional rationality demand? A first prerequisite is the nourishment and development of a rich life of the senses. "If we are to be full of life and fully alive," says Macmurray, "it is the increase in our capacity to be aware of the world through our senses which has first to be achieved."[10] For the healthy development of growing children especially, the importance of an environment rich in sensory experience—color, sound, smell, movement, texture, a direct acquaintance with nature, and so forth—cannot be too strongly emphasized. And that fine sensitivity in discrimination which is the heart of emotional rationality arises in working and playing with the materials of the senses—through storytelling, drama, movement, music, painting, handwork, encounters with responsible, involved other human beings. What is demanded is clearly an artistic education in which the senses are nourished and sensibility and sensitivity developed. The lack of such an education can produce only a society that, whatever its cleverness and power, becomes increasingly philistine, insensitive to life, and uncaring, because incapable of truly knowing. And it becomes more and more a menace to itself and others.

From this perspective, therefore, one important form of question is: What is the nature and quality of the sensory life encouraged by the computer? At what points and in what ways can the computer in education serve a vital, qualitatively rich feeling for life? At what points and in what ways will the computer in education only further impoverish and stunt the sensory experience so necessary to the health and full rationality of the human individual and society? And a prior question remains: What place does the nurture and education of the emotional life have within the theories and practices that presently dominate modern education with or without the computer?

Closely related to emotional rationality is the part played by *the image in thinking*. In an exclusive emphasis on the inculcation of utilitarian, operational problem-solving skills as the main task of education, the determinative role of the image in all thinking tends to be forgotten. As a consequence, thinking becomes tied increasingly to old, habitual—unconscious and unexamined—images, and fresh insight that alone can release logic from its habitual grooves and compartments and guide it into new paths becomes impossible. As the theoretical physicist David Bohm has noted in an earlier issue of this journal, new insight announces itself in new images (one recalls immediately, in this respect, Newton, Einstein, Kekule, Poincaré, among others). To be sure, the full meaning and implications of the initial images must be worked out through hypotheses, formal logic, and calculation. But formal logic, the exceeding great importance of which is not in question here, is, as Bohm has shown, even in science secondary to insight via images and is never the source of new knowledge. Formal logic and discursive reasoning not in the service of insight lock us all the tighter into our presuppositions and rigid mental compartments.[11] Images may be of many kinds (visual, auditory, kinetic, and so forth), and a rich, vital imagery and image-making capacity of the mind are essential for new insight.

It is particularly in relation to the centrality of the image in all thinking that much serious thought must be given to the appropriate educational use of the computer with its powerful but highly specific, and exceedingly limited, form of imagery.

This becomes even clearer when it is considered that not only insight but all thinking is guided and shaped by our images, and that the quality of our images determines the quality of thinking and its consequences. We must of necessity rely constantly on our mental images in our efforts to integrate and understand the world. Even those physicists who engage in so-called imageless mathematics are guided by deep-lying images of the nature of the world they are probing, and they must have recourse to explicit imagery every time they seek to embody their calculations in instrumentation and experiment.[12] David Bohm has written, "Indeed, one finds that physicists are not actually able just to engage in calculations aimed at prediction and control: *they do find it necessary to use images based on some kind of general notions concerning the nature of reality*" (and he adds that the images dominating physics today are highly confused).[13] The nature of our imagery and the health of our image-making capacities become all-important, for they will shape the kind of world we come to know, and the kind of world we come, thereby, to give ourselves. It makes all the difference whether our images are living, mobile, and fresh or dead, rigid, and habitual, whether they are more or less conscious or unconscious and, thus, likely to insert themselves unnoticed into our thinking, whether they are responsibly employed or wantonly chosen and applied irrespective of the consequences.

One of the most pervasive, probably the dominant, image of the modern mind set is that of the machine. It is certainly the case that science, and the scientism that has come to shape most people's view of reality, is dominated by an imagery that is basically mechanistic. "It is no exaggeration," R. C. Lewontin has recently written, "to say that most scientists simply do not know how to think about the world except as a machine."[14] This mechanistic imagery has been exceedingly powerful in our uncovering and coming to understand the mechanical, physical cause-and-effect dimensions of reality, but is it adequate and appropriate for understanding the whole of reality? Even the so-called life sciences are dominated by the mechanistic imagery that attempts to locate the secret of life in the inanimate. The noted biochemist Erwin Chargaff has spoken of what he calls "'the paradox of biochemistry,' namely, that biochemistry is helpless before life, having to kill the organism before investigating it." And he adds: "Biochemistry is, in fact, much more successful in practicing the second part of its composite name than in following the prefix."[15] This mechanistic imagery has made it possible to manipulate life with much success, and with some undeniably useful results, but that it leads to an understanding of life itself is highly debatable. For an understanding of a living world and its requirements for survival, do we not need—in addition to the mechanical—living, mobile images that alone can guide a living thinking?

Our images will eventually give us the kind of world we come to know through them. As Owen Barfield has put it, if we persist in an exclusive preoccupation with mechanistic images, we will get a mechanical world.[16] It is, thus, in the imaging capacity of the mind that we find the moral element at the heart of all thinking. We have a responsibility for the images we make and use in our efforts to integrate, understand, and shape the world. The development of a rich, healthy, living image-making capacity is the chief task of an education that is concerned with the development of a creative, responsible living-thinking, and of a living world.

This is what makes the feeling-life of the school-age child of paramount importance for education, for it is here that the education of emotional rationality and the education of a strong, vital image-making capacity are joined. It is in the picturing- and feeling-life of the school age child that the creative, image-making capacity begins to come fully into its own and to cry out for nourishment. The provision of an education rich in sensory experience and with opportunities for developing fine discrimination becomes essential for a living-thinking in which penetrating insight and strong logic undergird one another. The most serious questions must, therefore, be raised and weighed in considering the place of the computer in the education of young children.

We live at a time when the feeling, image-making capacities of the child have been already pushed aside and ignored in modern education by a misplaced emphasis on ever-earlier development of analytical, narrowly conceived functional skills. Are we in danger of now further subjecting the child to a technology that would seem to eliminate entire sources of sensory experience and living imagery—while accentuating out of all proportion images of a very limited type, all the while inserting the latter directly into the child's mind during its most plastic and formative years? What is the effect of the flat, two-dimensional, visual, and externally supplied image, and of the lifeless though florid colors of the viewing screen, on the development of the young child's own *inner* capacity to bring to birth living, mobile, creative images of his own? Indeed, what effect does viewing the computer screen have on the healthy development of the growing but unformed mind, brain, and body of the child?

The questions can be multiplied, and educators have a responsibility not to blink them nor to assume that they are not really urgent. As we grasp the issues involved, we will begin to see how important it is to realize that the alternative to sitting Canute-like before the incoming tide of electronic and computer technology is not to herd all the children onto the beach to have them bear the full brunt of the onrushing tidal wave. As for adults, we may come to see more clearly that the most important human problems are not computable, that besides data and calculation they require understanding, interpretation, and, often, empathy, sacrifice, and restitution.[17]

This issue of the *Record* is offered in the hope that it can encourage and make a contribution to a discussion that needs to be taken up and resolutely pursued. Only in such a dialogue can we begin to realize the full potential of the computer and of the human being alike.

Notes

1 For one such exception, see James W. Carey, "High-Speed Communication in an Unstable World: What Has Happened to Conversation and Discussion That Attempted to Cultivate Deeper Focus of Understanding?" *The Chronicle of Higher Education*, July 1983, p. 48.

2 John Lear has commented on this similar use of the automobile to assuage fears about genetic technology: "It is argued that anxieties about the future should be avoided. That argument would leave the future to chance. The future was left to chance at the time Henry Ford made the automobile a household commonplace. What have we now as a result? Fertile farmland paved over, closed to the planting of food crops. Rainfall runoff from the pavement periodically flooding sewage treatment systems and polluting streams we depend on for drinking water. The purity of the air we breathe polluted by automotive exhaust fumes. Sunlight acting on the fumes, generating smog and altering the climate around big cities. All of this ugliness might not have been foreseeable in Ford's day, but the logic of it is so straightforward that much of it surely would have been at least suspected, if possible sequelae of the motorcar's advent had been considered then along with the pleasures of personalized transportation" (John Lear, *Recombinant DNA: The Untold Story* [New York: Crown, 1978], p. 246; quoted in Liebe F. Cavalieri, *The Double-Edged Helix, Science in the Real World* [New York: Columbia University Press, 1981], p. 65).

3 See David Burnham, *The Rise of the Computer State* (New York: Random House, 1983).

4 See David E. Sanger, "Computer Makers Pursuing Campus Sales and Research," *The New York Times*, January 20, 1984, pp. A1, D18; David Noble and Nancy E. Pfund, "The Plastic Tower: Business Goes Back to College," *The Nation*, September 20, 1980, pp. 246–52; and Jonathan King, "New Genetic Technologies: Prospects and Hazards," *Technology Review*, February 1980, pp. 57–65.

5 See, for example, William Serrin, "'High Tech' Is No Jobs Panacea, Experts Say," *The New York Times*, September 18, 1983, pp. 1, 28; and Philip Matters, "High-Tech Cottage Industry, Home Computer Sweatshops," *The Nation*, April 2, 1983, pp. 390–92.

6 Joseph Weizenbaum, "The Computer in Your Future," *The New York Review of Books*, October 27, 1983, pp. 58–62.

7 John Macmurray, *Reason and Emotion* (London: Faber and Faber Ltd., 1935).

8 Ibid., p. 26.

9 It is in this latter connection that the computer is frequently recommended as educationally important for children in that "it motivates them." Motivation by itself, however, it should be noted, is not an educationally sufficient argument *for* anything. When motivation is lacking in education, we may be sure there is a problem. Where motivation is present there may also be a problem; there will certainly remain a problematical situation. Children can be motivated by many things—ice cream, sex, cash, for examples. In the hands of an enterprising behavioral psychologist each of these could no doubt yield some interesting classroom procedures, but we should presumably like to know more before introducing them *carte blanche* into the nation's schools.

10 Macmurray, *Reason and Emotion*, p. 40.

11 David Bohm, "Insight, Knowledge, Science and Human Values," *Teachers College Record* 82, no. 3 (Spring 1981): 380–402.

12 See "Science and Imagination: An Interview with John Davy," *Towards* 1 (Winter 1980–1981): 17–24.

13 David Bohm, *Wholeness and the Implicate Order* (London: Routledge & Kegan Paul, 1980), p. xiii (emphasis added).

14 R. C. Lewontin, "The Corpse in the Elevator," *The New York Review of Books*, January 20, 1983, p. 34.

15 Erwin Chargaff, *Voices in the Labyrinth: Nature, Man, and Science* (New York: Seabury Press, 1977), p. 89; also see Cavalieri, *The Double-Edged Helix*.

16 Owen Barfield, *The Rediscovery of Meaning and Other Essays* (Middletown, Conn.: Wesleyan University Press, 1977), p. 185.

17 See Joseph Weizenbaum, *Computer Power and Human Reason: From Judgment to Calculation* (San Francisco: W. H. Freeman, 1976); also see idem, "Limits in the Use of Computer Technology: Need for a Man-Centered Science," in *Toward a Man-Centered Medical Science*, ed. Karl E. Schaefer (Mt. Kisco, N.Y.: Futura Publishing, 1977), pp. 83–97.

Mindstorms in the Lamplight

JOHN DAVY
Emerson College, Sussex, England

In this short review, I shall attempt an evaluation of Seymour Papert's *Mindstorms*,[1] and the approach to the use of computers in education it embodies.

This commentary cannot be exhaustive. The virtue of Papert's work is that it is not trivial. It impinges on fundamental questions of education, psychology, philosophy, and epistemology, and a full analysis would require a much longer treatment. My purpose here, in response to the mainly enthusiastic and uncritical reception of *Mindstorms* by teachers and parents, is to sound a skeptical note, and to justify it.

Papert's achievement is to devise a programming language, LOGO, that enables children to construct their own programs, and to control a small robot, the turtle (or an equivalent on the video screen). They can make the turtle, for example, draw shapes. The kinds of things LOGO enables children to do with turtle embody "powerful ideas" (notably mathematical and physical ideas). Thus, says Papert, the child learns through doing, is in control all the way, has fun, and is ushered into the mathematical and computer culture with confidence. "The new knowledge is a source of power and is experienced as such from the moment it begins to form in the child's mind" (p. 21).

Papert is not naive about the potency of the realm to which he is introducing children. Computers are tools. Tools are never neutral, but create a culture of tool users who have to operate them on the tools' terms. Computers embody a mechanized version of thinking. Will they make children think mechanically? Papert's answer is yes, they will. But LOGO enables them to *choose* to learn to think in this way. "I have invented ways to take educational advantage of the opportunities to master the art of *deliberately* thinking like a computer. . . . By deliberately learning to imitate mechanical thinking, the learner becomes able to articulate what mechanical thinking is and what it is not" (p. 27).

The LOGO approach is underpinned by Piaget (with whom Papert worked for some time). But it is a "new" Piaget, setting aside his framework of natural development in favor of a more "interventionist" approach. In particular, it is claimed that LOGO makes it possible for children to "concretize" formal operations well before Piaget's threshold of eleven to twelve years. Furthermore, they can enter these realms with enjoyment, and avoid creating for themselves the blocks to mathematics that easily form at this stage because formal operations seem so remote from real life. In a world shaped by the powerful ideas of mathematics, we are told, the mathematical illiteracy engendered by such blocks must be overcome, and with the help of LOGO, children may be initiated early and painlessly.

I shall question this program on three grounds: its tendency to experiential impoverishment; its uncritical "head-start" philosophy; and its idolatry of "powerful ideas" and computer thinking. While Papert acknowledges, briefly, that there may be situations in which thinking like a computer is *not* appropriate or useful, he claims that by deliberately learning mechanical thinking, children will become aware that this is just one "cognitive style" and that they can choose others. He does not say what others he recognizes, or how children might learn to discover, practice, and value them. He merely glances sidelong here at issues of great importance, which I shall consider briefly at the conclusion of this discussion.

Leaving aside the theoretical underpinnings, what actually happens in a LOGO learning environment? Examples are given in the book. The child sits at a keyboard with a screen, typing instructions. With the help of LOGO, the machine is programmed to draw a "flower" (Figure 1), then a lot of "flowers" in a "garden" (Figure 2). Next, the child may devise a program to draw a bird (Figure 3), then a flock of birds (Figure 4). Then the birds can be put into motion. "The printed page," says Papert, "cannot capture either the product or the process; the serendipitous discoveries, the bugs, the mathematical insights, all require movement to be appreciated" (p. 93).

Now let's hold on a moment. Flowers? Birds? Movement? There is not a flower or bird in sight, only a small screen on which lines are moving, while the child sits almost motionless, pushing at the keyboard with one finger. As a learning environment, it may be mentally rich (even if the richness is rather abstract), but it is perceptually extremely impoverished. No smells or tastes, no wind or birdsong (unless the computer is programmed to produce electronic tweets), no connection with soil, water, sunlight, warmth, no real ecology (although primitive interactions with a computerized caterpillar might be arranged).

Granted, we are not discussing the teaching of botany, meteorology, or ecology, but the mastery of "powerful ideas." Yet the actual learning environment is almost autistic in quality, impoverished sensually, emotionally, and socially. (All right, children have fun, and sometimes work together on programming, a social and affective plus. But compare the scene with any traditional children's playground games, or their involvement in the ancient and wise psychodramas of fairy stories.)

In this respect, computers in classrooms are simply extensions of television in classrooms. Evidence of any profound educational value in television, except as an adjunct for good teachers (any profundity then comes from the teachers, not the television), is not known to me. It feeds us with brief stimuli and surrogate reality. All the energy that has gone into debating the effects of

BUILDING UP

Figure 1

Figure 2

IT'S A BIRD!

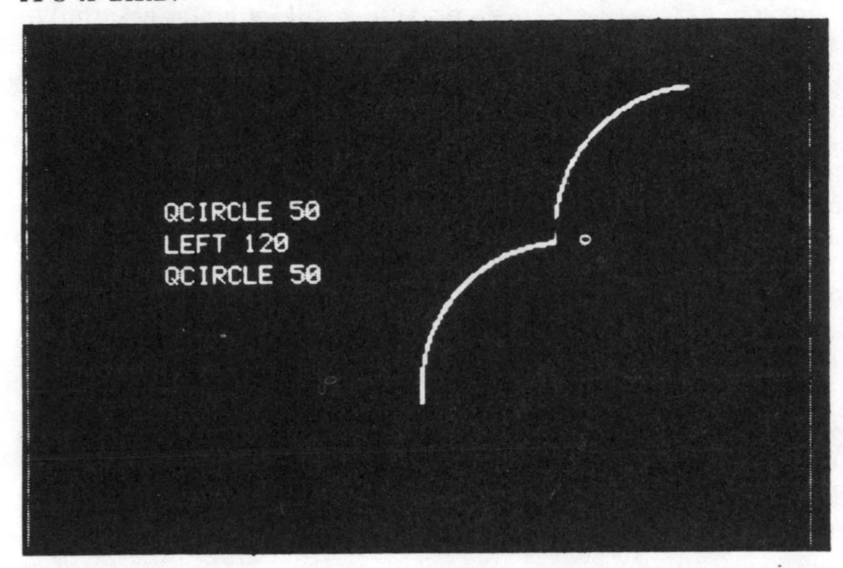

Figure 3

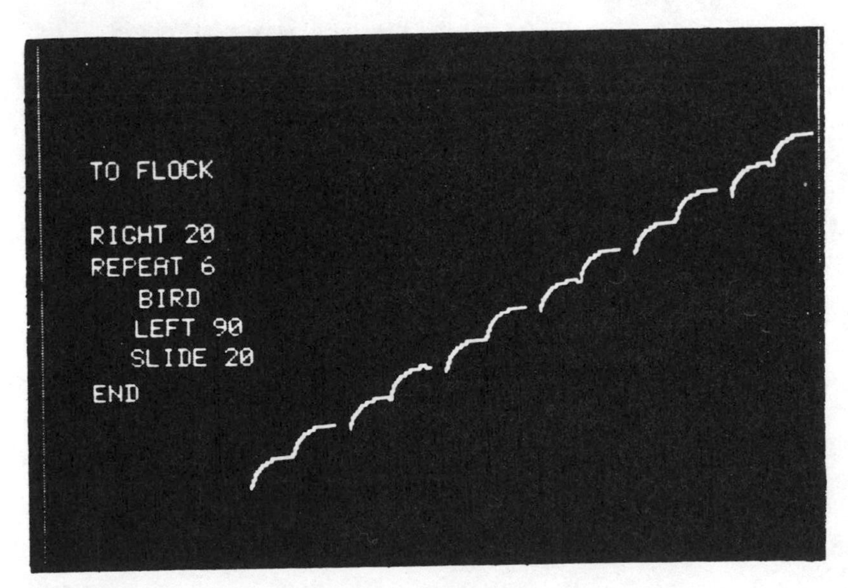

Figure 4

the content of television programs has obscured the question of sheer impoverishment of life, the effects of simply sitting still for hours, absorbed in an artificial image world.

Computers, of course, are not entertainment, but LOGO makes them entertaining as a means of introducing children to powerful ideas. These are the ideas that are really shaping adult life, we are told, so why not meet them early? Put away childish things like making sand castles, feeding real turtles, playing tag in a playground rather than on a video screen and with other children rather than an electronic mouse, collecting real flowers, painting with a real brush and paints. But if you do not learn to control computers early, the earnest voices whisper, they will control you. You must give your child every chance.

If I seem intemperate, it is because of the loss of real connection with childhood of which the whole temper of *Mindstorms* is a symptom. Papert himself cannot be blamed for this. He is a brilliant exponent and champion of the dominant cultural tide, technological and instrumental in spirit and soul. When he was two, as he describes in his Foreword, Papert knew the names of lots of automobile parts, notably from the gearbox and transmission. He soon became adept at turning wheels not only in the external world but in his head (and indeed in his heart: "I remember there was *feeling, love,* as well as understanding in my relationship with gears"). Gearwheel models later helped him into mathematics. It is a fascinating glimpse into the inner life of a man with a touch of genius.

However, there really is much else in childhood besides gearwheels. No doubt young Seymour did more than turn wheels in his head. And the focus of his book has been deliberately narrowed to the question of achieving earlier, deeper, and more effective entry into some powerful ideas of mathematics. But if adopted uncritically, the message of *Mindstorms* will reinforce the tunnel vision that afflicts education, servile as it is to technocracy and easily alienated from the fullness of human experience.

Piaget, of course, made his observations and discoveries in rather richer environments (although even he had to impoverish them a little for experimental purposes). His genius was to see deeply into largely spontaneous childish operations, and to draw out of the children themselves, through conversation, a glimpse of childhood consciousness. Like many important insights, basic Piagetian realizations are often fairly obvious once articulated. The childhood skills of managing seesaws and swings are exercises in applied physics. The physics is enacted, not thought; known intutively, not intellectually. Yet it is experience that can later be lifted into more abstract and conscious experience as a grasp of mathematical laws, calling for skills in formal operations.

The progress from sensorimotor through concrete to formal operations was regarded by Piaget as a real, natural developmental rhythm. Certainly, its unfolding calls for appropriate environmental correlates. In particular, the capacity for formal operations may scarcely develop at all if not exercised when it awakens around the age of eleven or twelve. But the idea that we are here dealing with natural developmental rhythms is challenged by Papert. As an "interventionist," he sees Piaget's stages as capable of being concertinaed into early childhood. LOGO allows us to introduce a first practice of formal operations to seven- or eight-year-olds. The computer way of thinking can thereby come "to inhabit the young mind," providing a head start in coping with the adult world.

The results of all kinds of head-start programs should in any case lead us to be cautious in expecting clear long-term benefits from meeting LOGO at age seven. It is too early for empirical evidence to exist, so the question must be left open. But even if positive evidence did exist, it should not lead us to neglect other questions. While Piaget explored some other aspects of development and education (for example, the child's relation to moral questions), his main focus was on cognitive development. And because most educational discussion is about cognition and intellect, this is what Piaget is best known for. Since even the most goggle-eyed computer enthusiasts scarcely argue for computers as tools for affective or moral education, Piaget can be summoned to support a case that is from the beginning a kind of caricature of what education is really all about.

In *Mindstorms,* Papert tells touching stories about children intimidated by mathematics, who then learned to love learning with the help of LOGO. Their love is for the machine and the games they can play with it, echoing Papert's own infant love of gearwheels. All this would be funny if it were not so sad. It is well known that autistic children can make close relationships with things that they cannot make with people. It could be interesting to explore whether LOGO might help some autistic children develop confidence enough to venture to play with people. But we are talking about pathologies and therapy, not education. What kind of a culture are we developing if people have to meet its most powerful ideas through machines rather than through people? If people—that is, teachers—consistently work in such a way that they block access to these ideas, should we not be looking at how teachers work rather than selling them a prosthesis? At the heart of real life is working with people, being with people, understanding people. (Does this have to be argued?) As long as classrooms include real teachers, cognitive development cannot, in the nature of the situation, be divorced from emotional, social, and moral experience. Particularly in the period before puberty, while engaged in Piaget's concrete operations, children are fundamentally involved, if they are in good health, in gaining social and emotional experience. It is prime time for imaginative and artistic education. Their relationships with adults at this time influence profoundly how they relate to adults in high school—including mathematics teachers. There are here very large areas of educational concern that are far more significant than demonstrating some kind of early competence in formal operations.

I should say here that I do not want to devalue computers in education altogether. That would be absurd and foolish. I take it as obvious that proper education in computer science belongs in high schools. LOGO will have real interest and value here. But there are further issues that need attention. LOGO is a sophisticated language, requiring considerable computing capacity. It may help entry into powerful ideas, but is it the best way to understand computers themselves?

Much has now been written about the ease with which we project aspects of ourselves onto these machines (and indeed, we really meet aspects of ourselves, notably our own capacity to "think like a computer," in the programs we use). The potential for obsession, delusion, and confusion is now well known, but no less a cause for concern for all that. The best medicine would surely seem to be proper insight into both the principles by which the machines operate and, still more fundamentally, the essential features of the "style" of thinking that computers embody and demand. For this, we need "transparent" systems, right down to the level of machine language. The force of development is to make sophisticated systems cheap enough for schools. There is little commercial incentive to sell transparent systems. But there is a significant intellectual interest and challenge. How can one open up for fifteen-year-olds the history of thought from which emerged Boolean algebra, information theory, the Turing machine? What tools would help? LOGO is, in its own terms, a brilliant achievement. But it uses this background to learn to operate within certain realms of powerful ideas. The interest in these is presented as power. The inner background, the spiritual choices that are actually being made when we think like a computer are not illuminated by playing with LOGO, since they are not grasped in any wider historical or cultural context.

Yet without concern for this context, LOGO and its like can only serve deeper idolatry of that "instrumental reason" which Joseph Weizenbaum, in his famous and penetrating polemic,[2] rightly identifies as one of the most serious illnesses of the computer age. Despite Papert's (unsupported) claim that early thinking like a computer will promote awareness of other styles of thinking, the entire temper of his work is in the spirit of instrumental reason. This is revealed very clearly in his argument that as learners, we are all fundamentally *bricoleurs*—structuralist jargon for "tinkerer"—assembling bits and pieces of materials and tools, which one handles and manipulates. Learning is learning to operate, to control, to be competent instrumentally. It is pragmatism in action. Truth is what can be made to work, the means are the ends. It is a tide of thought that runs so deep and strong through our technocratic society that one challenges it at one's peril. So it is worth looking at two more examples from *Mindstorms*.

To get a digital computer to draw a circle, one must break the curve down into many small straight lines. The LOGO program makes this explicit to the user. As Papert rightly says, this introduces children to the powerful idea of differentials. Essentially, this is the technique developed by Newton and Leibniz whereby continuous but variable processes can be mathematically grasped by breaking them down into infinitely small discrete steps. It is an abstract and very powerful method, a most fundamental tool in mathematics and physics. It is also a kind of essence of instrumental reason. With it, we can manipulate a biological growth curve mathematically. This can easily obscure the fact that if we "differentiate" an actual living plant, it will not grow any more. We have killed it.

Papert gives, in another context, the example of learning to understand the flight of birds. He argues that his approach is not ordinary reductionism, because we get nowhere with the problem by studying feathers. Our grasp of bird flight came from grasping mathematical aerodynamics and by building aircraft. By analogy, Papert argues that computer systems and artificial intelligence can "act synergistically with psychology in giving rise to a discipline of cognitive science whose principles would apply to natural and artificial intelligence" (p. 165).

This disguises the circular problem buried here. No one denies that computer systems can throw light on aspects of human intelligence. Quite obviously, the systems themselves are products of this intelligence, and so by studying them, we study aspects of ourselves. The emphasis needs to be on *aspects*. Leaving out, now, the emotional and moral questions touched on earlier, the very force and success of computer systems, and the powerful ideas of physics and mathematics, easily allow them to occupy the whole ground. We take a limited truth for the whole truth, because this particular style of thinking gives such power.

Our culture is quite extraordinary in this combination of idolatry of a particular kind of power, while floundering fundamentally in helpless anomie. A good part of the problem, in my conviction, lies in the tendency of instrumental reason to prevent our asking important questions. This can be illustrated by pursuing Papert's bird flight example a little further.

While Papert sees himself drawing on the structuralist tradition, in which we owe much to Piaget, his structures are those of received mathematics (more exactly, the "mother structures" of the Bourbaki school). There is no discussion of how complete a description of the universe might be based on these structures. They "work" for the realms of powerful mathematical ideas with which Papert is concerned. There is a structuralist version of reductionism going on here. This is the more striking in that some biologists, also concerned with things like birds and bird flight, and realizing that received Darwinism is preventing our asking a lot of rather important questions, are also looking to structuralism for new progress.

Yes, aerodynamics throws light on how bird flight is physically possible.

But such insights tell us nothing about why birds fly from place to place. Aerodynamics enables us to see more deeply into the "adaptations" of birds for flight. All living organisms are adapted in very "intelligent" ways to their environments. We have to expend much intelligence (using a form of intelligence closely allied to instrumental reason) to understand these adaptations. Yet the concept itself is quite problematic,[3] since the word presupposes a "niche," a keyhole for the key. But neither can actually be meaningfully defined without the other. At the same time, our functional biological questions easily obscure nearly all recognition of the fact that we actually have no understanding of biological forms in themselves. Birds are seen as devices for flying, whales as devices for the consumption of krill, but we lose sight of the question of why birds and whales exist at all.

Goodwin, Webster, and others have recently been arguing for a structuralist theory of *biological* form.[4] Such a theory would have its own "mother structures." Certainly, there would have to be some relationships with the Bourbaki structures, since the universe is coherent. But the mathematics for biological forms may be very different from the mathematics for computers. There is an important frontier of modern thought here, which can only be crippled if these exploratory apprehensions are seized, limited, and treated merely as tools for instrumental reason.

Computers, by their very nature, and whether operated with LOGO or otherwise, are potent training grounds for thinking about thinking in purely functional, operational, and instrumental terms. This is the explicit philosophy of what Weizenbaum calls the "artificial intelligentsia." Within this framework, *Mindstorms* is a powerful and significant contribution. My contention, though, is that its brilliance is the brilliance of the pool of light beneath a street lamp at night, which features in what is evidently Weizenbaum's favorite drunk joke: The drunk is searching for lost keys in the pool of light. A policeman asks him where he lost them. "Out there," says the drunk, gesturing vaguely into the darkness. "Then why are you looking here?" "Because the light's better," says the drunk.

If we are scientifically honest, the real mysteries of human consciousness are still shrouded in darkness. They do not cease to exist because we learn to operate brilliantly in a confined and tightly defined cognitive mode. Do we do our children any service by gathering them into the lamplight, and suggesting they forget the rest? The light is flat, and there is little room to move around. Compared to the mysteries of hide-and-seek among moving shadows, it is a limited world, and modern adults are not having all that much fun living in it. And suppose the real keys to our future are not in the pool of light, but somewhere out there?

Even in mathematics there are mysteries. High-level pure mathematicians tend to complain that the realm where new mathematics originates is obscured for most students by instrumental reason. They are taught to manipulate the tools—hardened specialized devices needed to operate at the level of definitions, axioms, notations. But their origins are more mysterious, intuitive. Mathematics used to be called "the Queen of the Arts." It is not the same world as that of flowers drawn step by step by an electronic turtle.

Mindstorms deserves every appreciation in its own terms. It is those terms I have questioned in this brief review, especially if they are treated, by implication or by default, as sufficient for education or for life. And if it seems that I am making a mountain out of a molehill—after all, *Mindstorms* is a short book, with a limited aim—it is because, if it is a molehill, it is sited on the slopes of the mountain of instrumental reason. And embedded in the issue of truth as power, or truth as wisdom, is a fundamental spiritual crisis of our time.

Notes

1 Seymour Papert, *Mindstorms: Children, Computers, and Powerful Ideas* (New York: Basic Books, 1980).

2 Joseph Weizenbaum, *Computer Power and Human Reason* (San Francisco: W. H. Freeman, 1976).

3 Richard C. Lewontin, "Adaptations," *Scientific American* 239, no. 3 (September 1978): 212-30.

4 G. Webster and B. C. Goodwin, "The Origin of Species: A Structuralist Approach," *J. Social Biol. Struct* 5 (1982): 15-47.

Microcomputers in Education: Why Is Earlier Better?

HARRIET K. CUFFARO
Bank Street College of Education

The discussion of microcomputers in education has become an arena in which one can learn a great deal about education itself. In explaining, describing, hypothesizing, and questioning what computers can or will do in education, statements are also made, implicitly or explicitly, about the purpose of education, teaching, the content of curriculum, and the nature of the learner. Educational discussions have been revitalized as the known, the taken-for-granted, and the usual are rotated and viewed from this new and different perspective. It is as though every aspect of functioning in education must be questioned and considered now in relation to this technology. In this article, I would like to consider the relevance of microcomputers to the education of children in the lower age range of early childhood—three-, four-, and five-year-olds.[1] Intrinsic to my perspective as an early childhood educator is the emphasis given to an organic, developmental view of children and their particular learning styles. This view serves as the context for the discussion that follows and is the link that thematically connects the topics to be discussed: an examination of the different types of programming activities and the variety of software available for these young ages.

Certain claims for microcomputers have been made so frequently that by now they have achieved the status of attributes. We "know" that computers "generate excitement in the learner," provide "immediate feedback" and opportunities for "individualized learning." They promote "social interaction." And, most compelling, in using computers children will learn how "to think." This familiar clustering of attributes, creating its own logic, often leads to stating that the child is in "control of his or her learning."

These seemingly new educational possibilities have been basic considerations in the thinking that has guided the planning of programs for young children for a long time. The materials commonly found in early childhood settings—paint, blocks, crayons, paper, wood, water, sand—are selected because they invite the active participation, experimentation, and impact of

The work presented here was supported by a fellowship from the Center for Dewey Studies and the John Dewey Foundation. I also wish to express my appreciation to Yvonne De Gaetano and Barbara Dubitsky for their thoughtful reading and criticisms.

the child. Their unstructured nature allows children to set their own agendas in learning and they are open to a variety of individual approaches. Classroom activities for young children are arranged to invite and promote social interaction. These materials, activities, physical and social arrangements, and the developmental perspective of early childhood educators come together to create an environment in which children are encouraged to formulate and reformulate their ideas and hypotheses about self and world. In and through their play, children reconstruct their experiences, make connections, and experiment with possibilities. The statements made about early childhood settings may be questioned just as claims about computers may be. In both instances, potential and possibility can be limited by the perspective of the people involved. Richness and variety can be standardized and packaged, and underlying principles can be overlooked. What is needed is clarity about what we do know and the questions to be asked. The order of our questions is important. If *how* is asked before *why*, we will be building on a shaky foundation.

Basic to the rationale of early childhood educators is the consistent attention given to the transactional relationship between the child's development and the content and planning of curriculum. It is just such a perspective that is evident in articles by Favaro and Barnes and Hill,[2] as they consider computer programming in relation to young children. Basing their view of the child on Piagetian research, they detail the cognitive abilities and characteristics of the preoperational child in juxtaposition to the skills needed for programming. Finding little compatibility, if any, in the match between abilities and necessary skills, they seriously question the introduction of microcomputers into the classrooms of three-, four-, and five-year-olds. Written from a different perspective, and focused on teaching these skills, articles and studies have appeared that describe programming activities with young children.[3]

What is striking in these articles is the degree of individualized instruction and the preparation and time needed to enable young children to engage in programming. The one-to-one attention and the extended preparation required serve to underline the gap that exists between the abilities of the young child and the skills needed for programming. Assuming that one would wish to expend the time and effort, a basic question remains: What self-generated problems/projects do young children have that they can bring to the microcomputer? The activity described most frequently in these articles, and usually suggested by adults to children, is the making of geometric shapes using LOGO. Countless hours are being spent in early childhood settings discussing, comparing, making, manipulating, examining these shapes, in words and action, and in a variety of situations. What further benefits or understanding do young children gain by creating these shapes on microcomputers, even if it is only a supplementary activity? Is it the logical, sequential ordering of commands that is desired? Is it the precision of the shape on the screen that is sought? Surely, regardless of the degree of their understanding, young children cannot deliver such graphic perfection. What does it mean to children to command a perfect square but still not be able to draw it by themselves?

The need for adult support and preparation can be circumvented in instant programs that can call up geometric shapes by simply pressing a key on the board. Touching the T produces a triangle, S a square, C a circle, and B will change the background color of the screen. Children are then able to arrange shapes and colors as they wish. To the observer of young children using these programs independently, what seemed to be happening primarily was the creation of a situation in which children were altering their usual television experience by causing things to happen on the screen, particularly the changing of background colors over and over and over again. In other, similar programs, by pressing keys the child can call up a variety of objects on the screen and then move and connect them. The simple pressing of keys by a child to make shapes, vehicles, houses, sprites, and colors appear and disappear, or to place them in motion, raises questions in relation to one of the essential and fundamental tasks of these ages—the gradual move away from magical thinking and the need to clarify the distinctions between reality and fantasy, actuality and desire. What is to be gained, for example, in calling up cars and garages on a screen and then trying to park a car in a garage? If a benefit is an opportunity to exercise eye-hand coordination, that must be weighed against the exacting precision and timing needed to arrange this placement on the screen. There is a further consideration. The child is not parking the car; it is the program, as directed by the child, that does it. Control is shared by the child with the program. Yet, at the child's level of understanding, the extent of the microcomputer's contribution to the happening is not apparent. This computer activity may be contrasted with a situation in which a child is "parking a car" in block play. Here, the child's eye-hand coordination must also contend with the qualitative, with the texture of the surface on which the car is moved, and with the fit between garage opening and car width. Such complexities do not exist on two-dimensional screens. The computer version of parking a car is action in a vacuum, motion without context, and with reality twice removed. The child's direct manipulation with concrete objects is in itself a representation that has reduced and simplified the task of a driver actually parking a car. The activities described thus far have implicit within them many collateral learnings that go beyond the specified aims of the activities.[4] It is the presence of these collateral learnings—the distancing and narrowing of physical reality, the magical quality of pressing keys, the "invisible" sharing of control, the oversimplification of process, the need for precision and timing—that merit great attention when thinking about young children's learning and the use of microcomputers.

Though self-evident, it is worth noting that the microcomputer also introduces a particular learning style into the school setting of young children—the familiar posture of television viewing. The added dimension of interaction with the screen is small compensation when one thinks of the usual large-muscle, full-bodied movements characteristic of young children as they interact directly with the environment. The price for entering the world of computer programming seems rather high for young children.

Turning from programming to the software available for these ages, one finds Mother Goose and Sesame Street characters along with butterflies, clowns, animals, shapes, and dazzling colors. Much of the content is comprised of skill-oriented activities such as letter and number recognition, one-to-one correspondence, and concept formation. Opportunities are offered for visual discrimination, eye-hand coordination, finding similarities and differences. The addition of musical notes and sounds introduces auditory cueing and discrimination to the skills being promoted. A good deal of this software requires an adult to interpret procedures and to assist in reading words, prompting the next move, and identifying the correct keys.

On the whole, skill-oriented software is very similar to workbooks in content, with the exception that these "workbooks" move. Animation is a familiar mode of presentation and much like the television programs children watch. The difference lies in the fact that the child can direct, within limits set by the program, the actions that occur on the screen. The question here is not "Why use a microcomputer?" but rather "Why use workbooks, animated or not, with young children?" Workbooks present skills in a symbolic, sequential manner; differing approaches to skill learning account for the variety to be found among them. Their diversity has not modified criticism of them as being, all too frequently, uninteresting and unchallenging in their standardization, and mindless, repetitious, and stereotypic. Putting them in motion does not redeem them. For example, workbooks and software exist that deal with directionality (right/left, above/below). Whether on paper or a screen, these two-dimensional representations are far removed from the situations in which directionality is learned and named. It is in interactions with the environment as children move self and objects through space, cope with obstacles, direct and position self and others in play, that they learn the meaning of these concepts.

Regardless of the colors, tunes, and entertainment approach of this software, the presentation of skills is more formalized, prescribed, and impersonal when contrasted with situations in which activities to promote the same skills are based on and grow out of the interests of individual children and their classroom situations. In such instances, process and product inform each other, and the content is relevant and responsive to children's lives. A time does come when the learnings derived from interactions in the physical and social world are transferred to a symbolic level. What must be remembered is the long stretches of time and the variety of situations young children need to "experience referents" before they can deal with them symbolically.

Another category of software—computer graphics—offers a variety of activities in which children can "paint," "draw," and "finger paint." Peripherals that bypass the keyboard such as joysticks, paddles, and Koala pads allow the child to function more independently once procedures have been explained. Ease is achieved through the additional hardware and the fact that graphics do not require a correct answer as does most skill-oriented software.[5] Computer graphics also pose questions. For example, in "painting" via the computer, the experience is reduced and limited by eliminating the fluid, liquid nature of paint. In this painting there are no drips to control or spills to mop up. Neither are there opportunities to become involved in the process of learning how to create shades of colors; gauging the amount of paint to be mixed; experimenting with and discovering the effects of overlaying colors; understanding the relationship of brush, paint, and paper, the effects achieved by rotating the brush and varying pressure, or how one gains control of or incorporates those unexpected, unintended drips. The possibilities for nuance, gradation, and the full-bodied movements of children as they paint are diminished. There is an absence of texture, of smell, a lessening of qualitative associations with the experience of painting. In the software available to young children, computer graphics have a "stamped out," standardized, "painting-by-number" quality. Though the design or arrangement of colors, lines, and forms will vary with each child, there is a quality of sameness in appearance, if only because the intensity of colors is identical. It is as though individuality is flattened by the parameters of the program.

The imagination of the child is present regardless of the material used, but the nature of the material influences and affects style and expression. For example, magic markers have affected both the experience of drawing and the look of it. Variety in color intensity, differing textures achieved by varying pressure, subtle shading—all possible with crayons—are difficult to achieve with magic markers. As with any material, the possibilities offered by magic markers and crayons are determined by their physical composition. The nature of the "material" in computer graphics is the program, and that is less accessible to the examination and understanding of the young child. Again, the line of inquiry is not whether microcomputers can or should be used for painting and drawing with young children. The question is: Why are these activities included in most early childhood programs? When that is answered, attention can then be turned to selecting those materials that can best realize these aims.

Materials comprise a large part of the early childhood curriculum; they are the means by which children pose and reflect upon their questions, the means by which they give form to and communicate their thoughts and feelings. The materials chosen to create the learning environment of young children may be seen as a reflection of the teacher's organizing structure.[6] They are a statement, in outline form, of the possibilities that can occur in that room, of the teacher's aims and understanding of young children. In educational settings that have consistently stressed the importance of experience, direct participation, and sensory exploration, the presence of two-dimensional screens, abstractions, and simulations is anomalous. Phrased in early childhood terms, what kind of a "material" is the microcomputer? The programming possibilities for these ages are minor and limited. It is difficult to think of one simulation activity that could be more meaningful to young children than their own dramatic play. As for software, what has been selected from the existing early childhood curriculum are those activities that are adaptable to the functioning of the microcomputer. The technology has determined the predominance of skill-oriented activities. (The repeated references to skill learning and task-oriented activities is not to imply that they are not a desired or significant part of the early childhood curriculum. They are. What is debatable is the manner in which such learning is to be approached and the context in which it occurs.)

Thus far, microcomputers have been viewed primarily as a supplementary activity. I question even that. Computers would not be simply a new addition to the curriculum. They have the potential to alter how we view children and their learning styles and to influence the content of curriculum. Earlier, I observed that the use of microcomputers was causing a rethinking of the known and taken-for-granted. As I observe the introduction of technology into early childhood settings, it occurs to me that it is the prevalence of computers in the adult world, and the increasing importance given to them, that is a determining factor influencing the choices being made in early childhood classrooms. I think that what we are encountering primarily is an adult agenda, the adult wish to have children enter the computer world as early as possible. It is the "earlier the better," the "they are here to stay" mind sets that are reshaping aims and influencing our understanding of children. Uncritical acceptance of these overused, hollow phrases is one of the ways by which we disempower ourselves and limit our choices. We must be clear and honest about the constructs we create to rationalize our work. Whom do they serve? Where will they lead? To attend to consequences is not to resist change. It can also be seen as giving thoughtful consideration to the meaningful connection between theory and practice.

Until now, computers have not offered young children opportunities for qualitative experiences, situations that can serve as catalysts to stir new possibilities and to awaken vision. At the young child's level of capability, the world of microcomputers lacks the permeability and flexibility to accommodate the kinds of problems that children spontaneously deal with at these ages, the questions that arise from daily encounters with people and things. It is possible that some future merging of sound and color, a technological kaleidoscope that may stir aesthetic sensibilities and move the imagination, will provide opportunities for experiences that can expand the child's world.

A situation does exist at present in which microcomputers can enrich the world of young children rather than narrow it. I refer to microcomputer use with children with certain disabilities. In such instances, computers may give the child expanded access to the physical and social world and bring it closer—even if indirectly—to be examined as it has not been before.

My consistent emphasis on direct experience is not meant to imply that young children using computers are not experiencing. They are. It is the quality of that experience and the accompanying collateral learnings that are being questioned. What may be added to what has already been noted is that analysis, definition, and logic do not suit every realm of knowing or state of being. Ambiguity, uncertainty, and the qualitative also are a part of knowing and living. It would be ironic if in introducing the microcomputer to young children—a tool with enormous potential for expanding capacity and learning possibilities—we end up limiting the range and quality of their experiencing.

It is when children move more firmly into functioning at the concrete operational level, at about age eight, that they are better able to take true advantage of the challenges that computers and programming may offer.[7] Much adult eagerness to have young children use computers is based on the belief that it will be impossible to function or to be employed in the future without such expertise or knowledge. Anxiety can obscure judgment. The young people of today who have manifested remarkable programming ability did not have years of practice or preparation with computers. What they did have were ideas—the problems and projects they created and brought to computers. It may be more pertinent to think about what is missing in our educational situations that has not permitted the abilities and imagination of students and teachers, which we are currently seeing, to surface. What other capacities are we not eliciting?

However the present technology is used, imaginatively or not, it appears that it will have an enormous impact on education. The nature and quality of this impact will continue to be debated particularly as descriptions of what computers can do meet the reality of their use in classrooms. Substantive questions will be raised[8] and generalizations will be differentiated as computer use is studied in relation to actual institutional structures, decision-making policies, and the details of the reality of social and educational contexts.[9] For the present, the enthusiasm over computers has given rise to some interesting phenomena. There is a striking openness in communication and the sharing of ideas. (I have wondered if the public, social nature of the screen, its accessibility to being shared in use and in viewing, has contributed to this atmosphere of openness.) Articles directly invite comments. Reviews of software ask readers to share their ideas and experiences. Networks have been created and newsletters circulated to extend support. The vulnerability of not knowing, of being a novice (a position not particularly comfortable for many educators), has become a shared experience.

In working with teachers, seldom have I seen such self-conscious awareness and analysis of what is involved in learning. Thinking about their own functioning with computers has given rise to insights and an empathic view of the learning process of children. Lines of distinction and of distance between and among parents, teachers, administrators, and students are becoming blurred as the possessors of computer knowledge and expertise appear at any level of the institutional structure. Equally interesting has been the attention given so early to some of the consequences of computer use in the schools. If these matters are seriously considered and acted on, we may not have to face a ton of commission reports and recommendations in the future. I refer to the concern over the long-term effects that will result from unequal access to computers as determined by gender and socioeconomic status;[10] the impact of business and commercial interests on education;[11] and the possibility of health hazards.[12] Questions and concerns will continue, generating a flood of research studies. One further comment about early childhood education that bears upon other ages as well: Whether or not microcomputers enter the early childhood classroom, they will be present in the lives of young children—in homes, the games that surround us, television advertisements. Their style of presentation—sounds, colors, speed, competitiveness—and the atmosphere they create will reach young children. When television appeared, teachers had to (and still do) contend with and give serious attention to the effects of television content and its mode of presentation on children's interests, their attention span and responses. The influence of this new presence must also be included in our planning as we think about teaching and learning.

The emphasis I have given to quality, to context, to connections and process, reflects my view as an early childhood educator as well as the influence of John Dewey's philosophy on my thinking. In 1929, Dewey commented on another technological innovation:

> The radio will make for standardization and regimentation only as long as individuals refuse to exercise the selective reaction that is theirs. The enemy is not material commodities, but the lack of the will to use them as instruments for achieving preferred possibilities.[13]

Educators must think long and hard and with the utmost clarity about the possibilities they choose to offer children.

Notes

1 The interest in computer use in early childhood education is recent and, judging by the number of articles that are appearing and the workshops and conferences to be held, rapidly growing. At the 1982 national conference of the major early childhood professional organization, the National Association for the Education of Young Children, there were four sessions or workshops on computer use. The conference, held in November 1983 in Atlanta, listed eighteen presentations, in addition to an all-day and half-day preconference seminar/workshop.

2 P. Favaro, "My Five-year-old Knows Basic," *Creative Computer* 9, no. 4 (April 1983): 158–66; B. J. Barnes and S. Hill, "Should Young Children Work with Microcomputers—Logo before Lego?" *The Computing Teacher* 10, no. 9 (May 1983): 11–14.

3 S. N. Hines, "Computer Programming Abilities of Five-year-old Children," *Educational Computer* 3, no. 4 (July/August 1983): 10–12; S. Reed, "On South Shore Drive: Two Professors and Their Two Preschoolers Share a Computer in the Family Room," *Family Computing* 1, no. 3 (November 1983): 57–59; idem, "Practicing What You Teach: An Interview with Professor Pat Dickson," *Family Computing* 1, no. 3 (November 1983): 60–63; and L. The, "Gee Whiz, Those Computing Kids," *Personal Computing* 6, no. 12 (December 1982): 58–67.

4 John Dewey, *Experience and Education* (New York: Collier Books, 1963; originally published by Kappa Delta Pi, 1938). In Dewey's words: "Perhaps the greatest of all pedagogical fallacies is the notion that a person learns only the particular thing he is studying at the time. Collateral learning in the way of formation of enduring attitudes, of likes and dislikes, may be and often is much more important than the spelling lesson or lesson in geography that is learned. For these attitudes are what fundamentally count in the future. The most important attitude that can be formed is that of the desire to go on learning" (p. 48).

5 Much has been said about the "nonjudgmental" nature of work with computers. A considerable amount of software, particularly if it is skill-oriented or drill-and-practice, involves correct answers. Correct responses are rewarded with smiling faces, rainbows, starbursts, musical notes that go up the scale, and an assortment of flashing, dancing, colorful reinforcements. Incorrect answers receive sad faces, Bronx cheers, musical notes that go down the scale, and messages such as "try again" or a repeat of the instruction. Positive or negative, these are judgments. Does nonjudgmental refer to the absence of affect rather than judgment? Does it refer to the anonymity maintained by the student using the computer? Even though a program may refer to students by name and keep a record of their performance, one is not "known" as he would be in human relating. There is a difference to be noted in programming. In that case, "judgment" occurs when the program does not run. In all of this, there is a distancing from human affect and contact. In a similar vein, it is interesting to note the words used to describe computers—nonjudgmental, patient, friendly, untiring. While affect is removed from the learning situation by terming it nonjudgmental, it is reintroduced by attributing human characteristics to the microcomputer.

6 A. M. Bussis, E. A. Chittenden, and M. Amarel, *Beyond Surface Curriculum* (Boulder, Col.: Westview Press, 1977). Through in-depth interviewing, the authors explored the "internalized assumptions and constructs about teaching" of the teachers in this study. In analyzing teachers' understanding of curriculum, a distinction was drawn between the "surface content of curriculum and a deeper level of organizing content—with 'surface' referring to the manifest activities and materials in a classroom and the 'deeper level' referring to the purposes and priorities a teacher holds for children's learning" (p. 4). One of the main points I am stressing in this discussion of microcomputer use with young children is that the relationship between surface curriculum and the deeper, organizing content be reciprocally informing. It is a transactional relationship between the two—a shuttling back and forth between the *why* and the *what, when,* and *where* of curriculum—that is sought.

7 G. Burns, "Children's Approaches to Programming: A Teacher's Perspective" (paper presented at the American Educational Data Systems Conference, Portland, Oregon, May 10, 1983). Burns describes work with eight- and nine-year-olds in his own classroom at the Bank Street School for Children. Microcomputers were introduced as part of a research project. The anecdotal material and the detailing of process in this paper are noteworthy. The Favaro article cited in note 2 also is useful in detailing the cognitive abilities of children at this age.

8 R. D. Pea and D. M. Kurland, *On the Cognitive Effects of Learning Computer Programming: A Critical Look,* Tech. Rep. No. 9 (New York: Center for Children and Technology, Bank Street College of Education, 1983).

9 K. Sheingold, J. H. Kane, and M. E. Endreweit, "Microcomputer Use in Schools: Developing a Research Agenda," *Harvard Educational Review* 53, no. 4 (1983): 412–32.

10 Equity issues in relation to socioeconomic level involve two basic factors: the availability of computers in a school, and the types of activities for which the computers are used—programming and/or computer-assisted instruction. The former involves financing, the latter the kind of learning opportunities to be offered to students. Further refinement of these issues is presented in the Center for Social Organization of Schools report, The Johns Hopkins University (vol. 1, no. 1, November 1983, 15 pp.). For example: "Predominantly minority elementary schools use drill-and-practice activities much more than they use programming activities with their students. In contrast, low SES predominantly white elementary schools teach programming to students more often than they use micros for drill work, even more, for example, than the high SES elementary schools do" (p. 4). Also see H. J. Becker, "Microcomputers in the Classroom: Dreams and Realities," Center for Social Organization of Schools, The Johns Hopkins University, Report no. 319 (March 1982, 76 pp.). Concern over the possibility that computer use will be predominantly a boys' activity has caused educators to think about the concerted effort needed to support and encourage the interest of girls in computers. Such affirmative action would complement similar work being done in the area of mathematics with girls. There is a company that has developed and is marketing computer materials for girls—RHIANNON/Computer Games for Girls. As their promotional material states, the games in their first series are "related to essential survival in various historical and geographical settings." Emphasis is on "integrated styles of thinking rather than the repetitive point acquisition of most computer games."

11 If only in passing, concern has been expressed over the influence of business interests on educational decisions—to what degree will the available hardware and software determine curriculum content? Obviously, school purchasing will be a market to court on the part of manufacturers, just as publishing contracts have been. News items such as the following concretize some of the questions being raised: "Atari and General Foods' Post Cereals recently launched a nationwide, multi-million dollar computer literacy program called 'Catch on to Computers.' [It is] designed to give all age groups a free hands on learning experience with computers. . . . The Catch on to Computers events are part of a national program offering computer hardware and software in exchange for proof-of-purchase seals from any brand of the entire line of Post Cereal brand." (*Electronic Education* 3, no. 2 [October 1983]: 55).

12 The health issues that have been raised still seem to be in the realm of possibility. Concern has been expressed, both in the popular press and professional journals, regarding possible physiological consequences of microcomputer use. The areas most commonly mentioned are eye and musculoskeletal difficulties and neurological implications. Considering the amount of time that might be spent with computers from the time of schooling through one's career, coupled with television viewing, these questions demand immediate attention. See *Harvard Medical School Health Letter* 8, no. 5 (April 1983): 1–5; Hearings of the Subcommittee on Investigation and Oversight, Committee on Science and Technology, U.S. House of Representatives (Washington, D.C., May 12–13, 1981); and *Bureau of Radiological Health Bulletin* 15, no. 6 (Monday, May 4, 1981): 1–2.

13 John Dewey, *Individualism Old and New* (New York: G. P. Putnam's Sons, Capricorn Books, 1962; originally published, 1929).

Computer Pedagogy? Questions Concerning the New Educational Technology

ARTHUR G. ZAJONC
Amherst College

At this point in the "computer revolution" one can do little more than speculate concerning the long-term benefits or detriments that may accompany the extensive use of computers in education. Yet if we are to use this technology responsibly we must not hesitate to frame critical pedagogical and ethical questions concerning the use of this or, indeed, of any new technology in education. Few things are more important for our future than the education of the young, yet in our rush to embrace a new fad we risk overlooking the long-term deleterious effects of what may appear to be a harmless or progressive new technology. I wish to ask a few of what seem to me to be the most significant questions regarding computer based instruction or education. Yet any such set of questions must be based, explicitly or implicitly, on one's view of the child and its maturation, emotional and volitional as well as intellectual. In attempting to pose a set of questions responsibly, I will make explicit the theoretical framework from which they arise. This article, therefore, falls into two parts. The first summarizes those elements of developmental psychology[1] that will later, in the second part, act as the matrix within which we may develop questions. The answers, the real answers, must await sensitive and careful research. But then should we not submit each of our educational initiatives to systematic theoretical and empirical scrutiny?

CHILD DEVELOPMENT

I begin with the explication of three aspects of Piaget's theory: accommodation and assimilation, cognitive structures, and development by stages. Once we have understood each of these concepts and their relevance to learning, the place (or misplacement) of computers in education gains clarity.

ACCOMMODATION AND ASSIMILATION

The polar processes of accommodation and assimilation form the logical center of Piaget's "genetic epistemology."[2] Although the newborn infant may completely lack all formal knowledge and, according to Piaget, all static "cognitive structures,"[3] the activities of accommodation and assimilation are sufficient to initiate cognitive development. Accommodation and assimilation can perhaps best be understood through their most vivid manifestations. In the case of accommodation, *imitation* serves this purpose, and in that of assimilation, *symbolic play* or *imagination*.

The process of accommodation is one in which the subject transforms or creates inner structures in order to accommodate a new object. This seems to be accomplished by a rehearsal, inner or outer, of the new experience. Piaget recognizes three levels of imitation: imitation through action, deferred imitation, and interiorized imitation. These provide the vehicle for the constitution of both operative aspects of thought and, through the last form of imitation, that of mental imagery. In the very young child the capacity for imitation, that is, pure accommodation, is present to an extraordinary degree. Not only is every aspect of the child's external environment an object of imitation, but also less tangible complexes of activities and emotions. The teacher's tender caress after a fall may turn up in endless variations, for example, as the comforting of a fallen doll or a wounded playmate. Thus are the moral, emotional, and aesthetic sensibilities of the child powerfully influenced by its capacity for imitation, for accommodation. Once one accepts the fact of accommodation, there arises the enormous responsibility for the educator to provide an environment fully worthy of imitation. Once again, I stress what should be entirely obvious, namely, that the objects accommodated should also be considered in their aesthetical and ethical dimensions. That is, the nursery should be beautiful, secure, and caring as well as instructional. In fact, as will become more evident later, the instructional component of early childhood education has essentially nothing to do with the teaching of conventional materials; rather, one should assist at this time in establishing the cognitive bases in the child for later and higher levels of learning. Thus the aesthetic and ethical dimensions become all the more important in the early years. In summary, child development hinges on the selfless capacity for imitation, that is, the ability to accommodate in order that something new can be absorbed from the environment.

Equally important is the complementary activity of assimilation, which Piaget defines as "the integration of external elements into evolving or completed structures of an organism."[4] When a child selects a nearby pine cone to become a loaf of bread, and a stone to be its knife, it is "assimilating" or integrating external elements (pine cone and stone) into an existing structure (domestic activity). Vigorous imaginative or symbolic play is an active projection of self. The whole world changes to serve the needs of the moment. Assimilation is an essential ingredient in development; it provides for continuity and, indeed, is necessary for recognition itself. Yet if it existed alone, no development could occur. The will and imagination to change one's world, whether in play or later through technological invention, must be coupled with the selfless capacity for accommodation. "Progressive equilibration" of these two processes is essential to intellectual growth, but it is not a static equilibrium. Rather it is a dynamic ebb and flow, a systole and diastole, a movement between receptivity and activity, between listening and speaking, which underlies cognitive growth.

COGNITIVE STRUCTURES

Out of the interplay of accommodation and assimilation arise what Piaget terms "cognitive structures."[5] Certainly the notion that all cognition, from ordinary perception to scientific discovery, depends on implicit mental structures is neither new nor unique to Piaget. The Romantic poets were filled with the idea that nature is an active agency that is constantly fashioning new organs of cognition in man, or cultivating those we have allowed to atrophy.[6] Goethe would write, "Every new object, well contemplated, opens up a new organ within us."[7] For our immediate purposes it does not matter at all whether we view the structures as innate but undeveloped (Chomsky and Fodor) or as constituted entirely by interaction with the environment (Piaget).[8] What is essential, however, is that we realize that education is concerned with the development of cognitive structures. Let us consider one such structure, its construction and its dependence on the feature of *action*—the structure of the "group of translations."[9]

Associated with the infant's gradually attained conviction that external objects possess an independent existence is his construction of a cognitive structure based on simple spacial coordinations. Geometrically these might be represented by such operations as: (a) AB + BC = AC; (b) AB + BA = 0; (c) AB + 0 = AB; (d) AC + CD = AB + BD. Through its own sensorimotor coordinations, and the experience accompanying them, the child maps out the laws of space. Perhaps this may first occur with the discovery of its own hand, or develop through a game of peek-a-boo. But gradually a cognitive structure is built up within the child out of its own actions that will allow it later to coordinate not only its own bodily movements but also its mental activities. Herein lies the critical point. Later cognitive activities rely on the development of suitable mental structures, and the construction of these structures is predicted primarily on action, not language. As Kurt Fischer writes in a recent article, "All cognition starts with action. . . . the higher-level cognitions of childhood and adulthood derive directly from these sensorimotor actions: Representations are literally built from sensorimotor action."[10] Piaget writes:

> From the most elementary sensorimotor actions (such as pushing and pulling) to the most sophisticated intellectual operations, which are interiorized actions, carried out mentally (e.g., joining together, putting

in order, putting in one-to-one correspondence), knowledge is constantly linked with actions or operations, that is, with transformations.[11]

Piaget and subsequent workers have focused almost exclusively on those inner structures associated with human cognition. I would like to suggest that there exist two other aspects of the human psyche that demand similar attention both by developmental psychologists and by educators. I will term these the aesthetic and the ethical dimensions of the psyche. We may ask about them the very same questions we have asked about cognitive development, but for my purposes I will simply assert that development of a balanced life of feeling and purposive moral action requires a similar basis in early aspects of the child's development. Furthermore, I would maintain that accommodation and assimilation play an important role in this arena also. If we would have a child act kindly to another, lecturing or explaining about moral conduct is to demand a formal operative capacity of the child that it simply does not possess. Clearly, one's actions should set an example worthy of imitation. Similarly, the cultivation of a balanced life of feelings depends on an environment in which the use of color, form, materials, song, all unite to create a surround that fills the child with a lively experience of the beautiful. As for ethical conduct, so also for the beautiful. To lecture the five-year-old on aesthetics is a commonsensical absurdity. Yet by ignoring its active counterpart, one creates a void in childhood that cripples the child for later experience, action, and knowledge in just that dimension. One task of education, then, is to cultivate faculties that will later allow for perception and discernment in the ethical, aesthetic, and intellectual domains of human experience. We may turn to a rather unorthodox source for good counsel in this educational matter. Plotinus, writing of beauty and the faculty whereby it is apprehended, writes in the Ennead, "Beauty":

> For the eye must be adapted to what is to be seen, have some likeness to it, if it would give itself to contemplation. No eye that has not become like unto the sun will ever look upon the sun; nor will any that is not beautiful look upon the beautiful. Let each one therefore become godlike and beautiful who would contemplate the divine and beautiful.[12]

The "structures" or more metaphorically the "organs" that are required for cognition and for aesthetic and ethical judgment form themselves through action, imitation, and assimilation during early childhood. The Greek triad of the Good, the Beautiful, and the True still retains its significance as an educational ideal even in an age of relativism.

It is against this vision of child development that we must examine the place of computers in education. Certainly if one *defines* education in an impoverished way as the transmission of information and skills, then different and lesser questions will arise. But one can maintain, as I would, that up to at least the age of seven years we are seeking to nurture those capacities or structures on which subsequent development depends. In this context the place of the computer in early childhood education must come under very careful scrutiny.

STAGES

Few aspects of Piaget's theory have undergone greater critical discussion than his conviction that cognitive development proceeds by stages relatively unaffected by teaching efforts. That there is a natural rhythm to the development of the child is also a principle of Waldorf pedagogy, one that largely determines the content and form of presentation used in their classrooms. While the problem is highly complex, I would like to use some of the concepts of Piaget and Fischer without entering into the debate as to exactly when certain mental operations or functions reach maturity. Nevertheless, my questions regarding the use of computers in education depend on a developmental scheme. It is my conviction that the vast quantity of empirical evidence supports such a view, although detailed knowledge of the psychogenesis of specific structures or operational skills may be faulty.

As is well known, Piaget recognizes three major periods: (1) the period of sensorimotor intelligence; (2) the period of preparation and of organization of concrete operations; (3) the period of formal operations.[13] Likewise, Fischer speaks of three "tiers": (1) sensorimotor, (2) representation, and (3) abstract.[14] The first of Piaget's periods lasts from birth through the second year. Here there is a "prefiguration" in action and spacial coordination of mental operations that will appear later. For example, "on a small scale and on the practical level, we see here exactly the same operation of progressive decentration which we will then rediscover on the representative level in terms of mental operations and not simply actions."[15]

The second period, of concrete operations, extends from two to about twelve years, and contains two subperiods—one of preparation but with only preoperatory structure, and a second of concrete-operatory structures. Here mental operations develop but are restricted to those that bear on manipulable objects. Only with the onset of formal operations at age twelve do we see the capability to manipulate verbal propositions and abstract logical elements.

Piaget maintains that these stages are relatively immune to acceleration through training. Others will disagree. More to the point, however, is not whether one *can* accelerate normal development of formal operational skills but whether we *should* do so. Here it is a matter of informed judgment based not on the short-term goal of intellectual prowess but on long-term objectives that will include social and emotional dimensions as well. The recent raft of studies, books, and monographs on the dangers of early schooling should certainly restrain our optimism that artificially induced precocity yields long-term benefits.[16] If we can restrain our arrogance and allow ourselves to be guided by the child itself, then our task as educators should be to cultivate those facets of the child's nature that are critically active at that time. For example, in the first years when action, imitation, and imagination (or symbolic play) are vitally important, the child should not be set at a desk and drilled. Play should be allowed full space and encouragement. The objects of the nursery should be as simple as possible to enhance and even demand imaginative action (assimilation). A primitive doll made of a knotted handkerchief is infinitely superior to the usual explicitly membered and painted dolls replete with sounds, bed-wetting, and microprocessor control.

With these considerations we (at last) encounter certain of my fundamental concerns about computers in education. In our enthusiasm to do whatever is possible we neglect, as Weizenbaum writes, to ask whether we *should*.[17] By providing so completely for our children, do we not deprive them of their most creative faculties? By creating images for them, whether through television or a rouged doll's face, we still the imagination and blunt the senses. Waldorf nursery teachers constantly remark on the difference between "T.V. children" and those without television in the home. T.V. children do not know how to play, they cannot imagine what to do. If they are shown something to do, they perform it mechanically, without variation. It often takes months before the pine cone becomes a loaf of bread.

Let us ask this same question of the computer. Will it subvert or usurp, through its own extraordinary power, those capacities we should be seeking to cultivate in the young?

COMPUTERS IN EDUCATION

I should begin by making it completely clear that I am not a flat-earther. In my work as a physicist and teacher I use computers, large and small, constantly—whether to interactively run complex experiments in laser spectroscopy, to perform calculations, or to write this article. Perhaps because of this, the "mystique" of the computer has faded the more I have grown to respect its usefulness. The idiocy of those who maintain that one must start young to master the machine can be explained only by their complete unfamiliarity with computers. It is not a piano, which demands years of training and practice to operate. Especially as more and more effort goes into making programs or canned packages "user friendly," the computer becomes increasingly easy to use. This is not to imply that no intellectually exciting horizons exist in computer science, but that is an entirely different question.

Let me also say that I see little harm in encouraging adolescents (older than about twelve years) to use the computer. I would hasten to add that any curriculum should be balanced with vigorous programs in more traditional subjects including the arts, but this is obvious. My questions primarily concern the child at those stages of development before the "abstract" or formal operation period, that is, before the age of twelve.

We are used to hearing complaints about computers' replacing the teacher. As serious as this is, *my primary concern is that the computer may replace the growing child*. Consider the various components of any computer system: the central processing unit (CPU), the memory, and an input-output (I-O) device. Imagine the most powerful computer you care to: The CPU runs at blazing speed, the memory is practically infinite, and the I-O device is the most sophisticated touch-screen, color-graphics unit conceivable. Now add to this impressive hardware the software that certainly will one day be possible. It is a completely conversational and interactive language cueing not only on keystrokes, but perhaps on verbal or gestural commands. In one scenario this might be utopia for a computer-based pedagogy. To me it presents the problems in their most intense form.

The computer is like a fragmented projection of the human psyche. Each of its functions replaces one of our own. Just as we have replaced the child's active imagination (that is, the exercise of assimilation) through television imagery and certain toys, so the computer has the potential to replace nearly all the mental functions of the child. For example, memory has been found to be an essential factor in the successful operation of transitivity (A = B, B = C, so A = C).[18] We may possess the ability to perform this operation, but be prevented from doing so by an inability to retain all the elements in memory. The development of this operational ability depends, therefore, indirectly on the strengthening of memory. Reliance on an external device—the computer—can easily weaken that faculty. I would maintain that entirely similar arguments can be made with regard to the computational and logical functions of the CPU and program elements. These can replace and thereby undermine the development of corresponding faculties in the child. If the capacity to imagine has been undercut by television, interactive computer graphics threatens to complete the assault. Simply by pressing a button the child can transform his visual field at will. The use of language is here intentional, for there is clearly *no will* involved. The child is a passive doodler in such a situation, captivated by the images it can apparently create. But there is *no creation* here either. All these activities have been usurped by the machine. No one would contend that physical therapy is obsolete because the wheelchair has been invented. Neither should the computer be allowed to assume those functions that act as the foci for child development just because it can do so.

We may now profitably turn to another of the points discussed earlier—action. Piaget and others constantly stress that later mental operations are interiorizations of earlier sensorimotor activity. This has been a basic tenet of Waldorf pedagogy for over sixty years. Waldorf teachers, following Steiner's suggestions, commonly have their students run a triangle before proving that the sum of its interior angles is 180 degrees. Seymour Papert in his book *Mindstorms* recognizes this element fully.[19] In order to do "turtle geometry," one should *walk* the pattern. By observing what the body does we have the basis for both a concrete representation and later the formal or abstract description of that operation. The learning of represented and abstract operations must be based in action. But the computer distances us from action. It may assist in the development of formal operative functions, but it fundamentally interferes with learning at previous levels. We first execute geometry and mathematics through the coordinated activity of the body. The natural transition to the concrete or representational stage can be provided simply by pencil, paper, compass, and straight-edge. The equipment should be kept minimal, never intruding or exercising its own volition. The straight line should be drawn by the child, not the computer. Once again turtle geometry ultimately usurps important activities essential for the child's cognitive development. The turtle moves, not the child.

I have written about the computer as potential usurper of actions and assimilation, processes necessary for childhood development. I shall finish by considering that extraordinarily important function accommodation, which, as I described, is responsible for the formation of new cognitive structures. Moreover, I maintained that it is responsible also for the formation of aesthetic and moral structures. In truth these three are inseparable aspects of the process of accommodation. When the child imitates it cannot filter out the cognitive component of the lesson from its aesthetic and moral aspects. It imitates the whole, and the whole should be worthy of imitation. Yet the use of the computer is predicated on the assumption that cognitive structures can be cultivated in an aesthetically and ethically neutral environment. This is pure illusion. "No values" is just as much an ethical system as one that gives full conscious attention to them.

We must ask, in what sense can the child imitate a computer or its display? A pictorial answer is perhaps provided by the video-game imitations that fill current childhood behavior. The sounds and movements of Pac-Man become the movements of play. As much as I love technology, this image fills me with revulsion. On a less visceral level we may query after the cognitive structures we hope to induce via computer. If we learn, as Piaget maintains, through interaction of subject and object, indeed through actions in which "subject and objects are fused,"[20] if new structures depend on the profound imitative capacity of childhood, in what sense can computers teach? Shall small children mimic CRT displays? Are the structures thereby induced the ones we wish to fill our society?

Put simply, the world of childhood, environment and teacher, should be filled with the movements, patterns, emotions, images, and actions that, when transformed, should underlie adult intellectual, emotional, and moral life. By attempting to neglect the inevitable presence of the latter two, and by inserting what is properly a device involving formal operations into earlier periods of child development, we risk doing violence to the orderly and natural course of child development. Time and again, we have attempted to outdo, speed up, or improve on nature. Technological advance is predicated on our ability to do so. Yet we *must* ask what *should* be done, what in the light of our best understanding of child development is an appropriate use of a powerful technology, and what is inappropriate.

Notes

1 As will be evident, I draw heavily on the discoveries and views of Piaget, and also from the fundamental pedagogical principles underlying Waldorf education. See, for example, Jean Piaget, "Piaget's Theory," in *Handbook of Child Psychology*, 4th ed., ed. Paul H. Mussen (New York: John Wiley, 1983), vol. 1, pp. 103–28; and A. C. Harwood, *The Recovery of Man in Childhood: A Study in the Educational Work of Rudolf Steiner* (Spring Valley, N.Y.: Anthroposophic Press, 1958). For a description of child development that relates these two approaches, see Eva Frommer, *Voyage through Childhood into the Adult World* (Oxford: Pergamon, 1969).

2 Piaget, "Piaget's Theory," pp. 106–09.

3 Here Piaget differs with Fodor and Chomsky, who maintain the presence, in some form, of innate structures. The distinction is not important for my argument. Regarding this debate see M. Piatelli-Palmarini, ed., *Language and Learning: The Debate between Jean Piaget and Noam Chomsky* (Cambridge, Mass.: Harvard University Press, 1980). See also R. Gelman and Renee Baillargeon, "A Review of Some Piagetian Concepts," in *Handbook of Child Psychology*, ed. Mussen, vol. 3, p. 217.

4 Piaget, "Piaget's Theory," p. 106.

5 Ibid., pp. 120–25.

6 A. G. Zajonc, "Facts as Theory: Aspects of Goethe's Philosophy of Science," *Teachers College Record* 85, no. 2 (Winter 1983): 251–74; and idem, "Goethe's Theory of Color and Scientific Intuition," *American Journal of Physics* 44 (1976): 327–33.

7 J. W. Goethe, "Bedeutende Fördernis durch ein einziges geistreiches Wort," in *Goethes Werke*, vol. 13, ed. D. Kuhn and R. Wankmuller (Hamburg: Christian Wegner Verlag, 1955), p. 38.

8 See note 3.

9 Piaget, "Piaget's Theory," pp. 104–05.

10 K. Fischer, "Theory of Cognitive Development," *Psychological Review* 87 (1980): 481.

11 Piaget, "Piaget's Theory," p. 104.

12 *The Essential Plotinus*, trans. Elmer O'Brien (New York: New American Library, 1964), p. 43.

13 Jean Piaget, *The Child and Reality*, trans. Arnold Rosin (Middlesex, England: Penguin, 1976), chap. 3.

14 Fischer, "Theory of Cognitive Development," p. 481.

15 Piaget, *The Child and Reality*.

16 For example, Raymond S. Moore and Dorothy N. Moore, *Better Late than Early* (Pleasantville, N.Y.: Readers Digest Press, 1975); idem, *School Can Wait* (Provo, Utah: Brigham Young University Press, 1979); and Neil Postman, *The Disappearance of Childhood* (New York: Delacorte Press, 1982).

17 Joseph Weizenbaum, *Computer Power and Human Reason* (San Francisco: W. H. Freeman, 1976).

18 P. E. Bryant and T. Trabasso, "Transitive Inference and Memory in Young Children," *Nature* 232 (1971): 456–58.

19 Seymour Papert, *Mindstorms: Children, Computers, and Powerful Ideas* (New York: Basic Books, 1980).

20 Piaget, "Piaget's Theory," p. 104.

Putting Computers in Their Proper Place: Analysis versus Intuition in the Classroom

HUBERT L. DREYFUS, STUART E. DREYFUS
University of California, Berkeley

True computer literacy is not just knowing how to make use of computers and computational ideas. It is knowing when it is appropriate to do so.
—Seymour Papert, *Mindstorms*

INTRODUCTION

No one doubts that computers will play a rapidly increasing role in education. And almost no one doubts that this will be a great boon for students and teachers. But this rush to computerize the classroom has bypassed the basic question: In what areas can computers help and in what areas could the use of computers prove counterproductive? Just what is the proper place of computers in education?[1]

A few years ago Teachers College Press published a valuable book, *The Computer in the School,* edited by Robert Taylor, which organized the possible roles the computer might take under the rubric: tutor, tool, and tutee, and presented the views of experts on the virtues of the computer functioning in each of these modes. As tutor the computer could perform a continuum of tasks from drilling students in subjects where rote learning was necessary, such as arithmetic, spelling, or grammar, to taking the learner step by step through a domain of knowledge such as physics, asking the appropriate questions at each stage and checking the student's understanding before going on to more complex subjects. As tool the computer could serve as word processor, design manipulator, and so forth, and so enable students, like professional writers and designers, to work more transparently and efficiently in the medium of their choice. Finally, as tutee, the computer could be programmed by the learner to exhibit geometrical, algebraical, and physical relationships. In the process the student as programmer would learn programming as well as gain a feeling for relationships in some particular domain.

In each of these areas much good work has been done. John Seeley Brown's use of the computer to tutor subtraction, and to diagnose and classify over ninety subtraction bugs, shows the power of the computer to facilitate the acquisition of skills that involve acquiring, debugging, and following strict rules. In the second area, work with word processors and design systems has

An extended version of this article will appear as a chapter in a book by the Dreyfuses, Putting Computers in Their Place, *to be published in 1985.*

been making great progress and offers the advantage of any improved tool enriching human capacities. In using the computer as tutee, Seymour Papert has been the pioneering figure, having introduced a new language, LOGO, and a whole philosophy of education in which a child can develop the rational thinking necessary for programming and at the same time develop a feeling for geometrical and logical relationships by actually creating them.

Reading the literature, one gets the impression that the success of computers in each of these modes can be extended indefinitely to wider and wider domains and more and more sophisticated skills with increasingly positive results. This kind of continuum thinking, which Yehoshva Bar-Hillel once called the first-step fallacy in artificial intelligence (AI), has always been characteristic of work on computer intelligence. As subsequent problems and stagnation in AI have shown, however, such optimism must always be controlled by a specific look at what has been done and what more can be done.[2] In education this means asking what sorts of skill and what levels of skill can and should be taught using computers.

Making useful computer tools and teaching children how to use them seems to us unproblematic. Here, more can always be done and more is clearly better, so we will not discuss this area further. The first and third areas, the use of the computer as tutor and as tutee, however, exhibit the combination of success in limited domains and the tendency to overgeneral claims on the basis of these successes that must be watched. Attempts to use computers as tutors suffer from exactly the same difficulties that have beset the attempt to make computers generally intelligent, and the psychological assumptions underlying the use of computer as tutee are the same assumptions that give rise to the unjustified belief that expert systems will someday outperform the experts.

The failure to raise the question of the proper place of the computer as tutor and tutee, as if its place were obvious, rests on a deep unquestioned assumption expressed, as if self-evident, in the introduction to Taylor's anthology: "Despite the extensive innovation in computing, much remains the same—particularly in the way computer logic structures are related to human thought structures."[3] Since nothing more is said of the way human and computer thought structures *are* related, one gets the impression that they are umproblematically similar and this is a beacon to guide us in a rapidly changing field. This view is not new. Since the Greeks invented logic and geometry, the idea that all reasoning might be reduced to some kind of calculation has fascinated most of the Western tradition's rigorous thinkers. Socrates was the first to give voice to this vision. In the dialogue *Euthyphro*, Socrates demands of Euthyphro, an Athenian prophet who, in the name of piety, is about to turn in his own father for murder: "I want to know what is characteristic of piety which makes all actions pious . . . that I may have it to turn to, and to use as a standard whereby to judge your actions and those of other men."[4] Socrates is asking Euthyphro for what modern expert system builders would call a heuristic rule—a procedure that enables a computer or a person to make the right decision in a particular type of situation most of the time.

Instead of giving Socrates his piety-recognizing heuristic, Euthyphro does just what every expert does when cornered by Socrates. He gives him examples from his field of expertise, in this case situations in the past in which men and gods have done things everyone considers pious. Socrates persists throughout the dialogue in demanding that Euthyphro tell him his rules, but although Euthyphro claims he knows how to tell pious acts from impious ones, he will not give Socrates the rules that generate his judgments.

Plato tried to account for such difficulties. According to Plato, all knowledge must be stateable in explicit definitions that anyone can apply. If one could not state his know-how in explicit instructions—if his knowing *how* could not be converted into knowing *that*—it was not knowledge but mere belief. According to Plato, cooks, for example, who proceed by taste, craftsmen who use intuition, poets who work from inspiration, and prophets, like Euthyphro, who preserve the tradition have no knowledge; what they do does not involve understanding and cannot be understood or taught. Real knowledge is rule-governed and can be taught by making the rules explicit by dialectic, which consists in formulating the rules and then using counter-examples to debug them. What cannot be stated explicitly in precise instructions—all areas of human thought requiring skill, intuition, or a sense of tradition—are relegated by Plato to some kind of arbitrary fumbling.

The belief that such a total formalization of knowledge must be possible was only one strain in Plato, but it gradually came to dominate Western thought. Hobbes was the first to make it fully explicit. "When a man *reasons*, he does nothing else but conceive a sum total from addition of parcels," he wrote, "for REASON . . . is nothing but reckoning."[5]

It remained only to work out the univocal parcels or "bits" with which this purely syntactic calculator could operate. Leibniz, the inventor of the binary system, dedicated himself to working out the necessary unambiguous formal language. With this powerful new tool, the skills Plato could not formalize, and so treated as confused thrashing around, could be recuperated as theory. In one of his "grant proposals"—his explanations of how he could reduce all thought to the manipulation of numbers if he had money enough and time—Leibniz makes an important claim that finally brings all forms of knowing under the computer paradigm:

> The most important observations and turns of skill in all sorts of trades and professions are as yet unwritten. This fact is proved by experience when passing from theory to practice we desire to accomplish something. *Of course, we can also write up this practice, since it is at bottom just another theory more complex and particular.*[6]

Leibniz had only promises, but in the work of George Boole, a mathematician and logician working in the early nineteenth century, his program came one step nearer to reality. Like Hobbes, Boole supposed that reasoning was calculating, and he set out to "investigate the fundamental laws of those operations of the mind by which reasoning is performed, to give expression to them in the symbolic language of a Calculus.[7] So we arrive at the self-evident view that computers and people are alike rule-following, symbol-manipulating, rational beings. One assumes what has come to be called the information-processing model of the mind, and proceeds from there. That is just what people have been doing for years in the fields of AI and knowledge engineering—and are now doing in attempting to use the computer as tutor.

The same information-processing model of the mind lies behind the idea of using the computer as tutee. There, instead of assuming that the teacher's knowledge is a program one wants to make explicit and put into a computer so as to pass it on to the student, the student is supposed to acquire knowledge, that is, a program, in the process of programming the computer. Coming to understand and learning to program are the same thing. As Taylor puts it:

> To use the computer as *tutee* is to tutor the computer; for that, the student or teacher doing the tutoring must learn to program, to talk to the computer in a language it understands. The benefits are several. First, because you can't teach what you don't understand, the human tutor will learn what he or she is trying to teach the computer. Second, by trying to realize broad teaching goals through software constructed from the narrow capabilities of computer logic, the human tutor of the computer will learn something both about how computers work and how his or her own thinking works.[8]

Programming the computer in domains such as math and physics—and, in principle, in any domain in which intuition and knowledge are the goal—consists in learning to think procedurally, like a computer. One learns by acquiring and debugging a mental program. Seymour Papert is the best exponent of this computational model of human thinking, which he calls the epistemological view. Like Leibniz, he thinks that even physical skills are implicit theories. "Our strategy," he tells us, "is to make visible even to children the fact that learning a physical skill has much in common with building a scientific theory."[9]

Papert notes that "many people will argue that overly analytic, verbalized thinking is counterproductive even if it is deliberately chosen."[10] But he does not take this "flimsy" objection seriously. Why should he? In our culture such objections are made by soft-headed humanists or mystical defenders of ineffable intuitions, and the battle against them was won by procedural thinkers at the time of Socrates and Plato. Unless one can provide a positive alternative to the dominant view that to learn is to acquire a program, it follows logically that programmed tutors can and should replace human ones and that one should also use the computer as tutee so that the student perfects his ability to think procedurally like a computer. Moreover, both techniques can and should be generalized to all areas of education, even the playground.

If we are to see the limits of this view we must question the assumption that computers and people have similar thought processes—that learning a skill is merely acquiring a step-by-step procedure. This is to fly in the face of a tradition that seems to be based on solid evidence. Philosophers and psychologists have, indeed, accurately described skills at the moment when these skills became conspicuous. Unfortunately, we become aware of our mastery of some skill only when things are not going smoothly, or when someone has given us a laboratory task in which we have no prior experience, and thus no appropriate skill. Then we are, indeed, dependent on analysis. However, to let the phenomena of everyday, successful, skilled activity show itself as it is, we will have to describe what the tradition has passed over: what happens as one learns, both from instruction and experience, to act appropriately in a familiar domain. In attempting such a phenomenological description we must be prepared to abandon the traditional view that a beginner starts with specific cases and, as he becomes more proficient, abstracts and interiorizes more and more sophisticated rules; that, as Papert puts it, experience in particular situations is necessary only to improve the rules, "to trap and eliminate bugs."[11] It might turn out that skill acquisition moves in just the opposite direction: from abstract rules to particular cases. Let us see.

A FIVE-STAGE MODEL OF SKILL ACQUISITION

STAGE 1: NOVICE

Normally, the instruction process begins with the instructor's decomposing the task environment into context-free features that the beginner can recognize without benefit of experience. The beginner is then given rules for determining actions on the basis of these features, like a computer following a program. The beginning student wants to do a good job, but lacking any coherent sense of the overall task, he judges his performance mainly by how well he follows his learned rules. After he has acquired more than just a few rules, so much concentration is required during the exercise of his skill that his capacity to talk or listen to advice is severely limited.

For purposes of illustration, we shall consider two variations: a bodily or motor skill and an intellectual skill. (The reader wishing to see examples of the process we shall outline taken from an interpersonal skill more akin to teaching [namely, nursing] should consult Patricia Benner's "From Novice to Expert."[12]) The student automobile driver learns to recognize such interpretation-free features as speed (indicated by his speedometer) and distance (as estimated by a previously acquired skill). Safe following distances are defined in terms of speed; conditions that allow safe entry into traffic are defined in terms of speed and distance of oncoming traffic; timing of shifts of gear is specified in terms of speed; and so forth. These rules ignore context. They do not refer to traffic density or anticipated stops.

The novice chess player learns a numerical value for each type of piece regardless of its position, and the rule "always exchange if the total value of pieces captured exceeds the value of pieces lost." He also learns that when no advantageous exchanges can be found, center control should be sought, and he is given a rule defining center squares and one for calculating extent of control. Most beginners are notoriously slow players, as they attempt to remember all these rules and their priorities.

STAGE 2: ADVANCED BEGINNER

As the novice gains experience by actually coping with real situations, he begins to note, or an instructor points out, perspicuous examples of meaningful additional components of the situation. After seeing a sufficient number of examples, the student learns to recognize them. Now, in addition to the *rules*, which apply to objectively defined *nonsituational features* recognized by the novice, instructional *maxims* can refer to these new *situational aspects* recognized on the basis of experience. The advanced beginner confronts his environment, seeks out features and aspects, and determines his actions by applying rules and maxims. He shares the novice's minimal concern with quality of performance, instead focusing on his adherence to the principles defining correct action. The advanced beginner's performance, while improved, remains slow, uncoordinated, and laborious.

The advanced beginner driver uses (situational) engine sounds as well as (nonsituational) speed in his gear-shifting rules, and observes demeanor as well as position and velocity to anticipate behavior of pedestrians or other drivers. He learns to distinguish the behavior of the distracted or drunken driver from that of the impatient but alert one. No number of words can serve the function of a few choice examples in learning this distinction. Engine sounds cannot be adequately captured by words, and no list of objective facts about a particular pedestrian enables one to predict his behavior in a crosswalk as well as can the driver who has observed many pedestrians crossing streets under a variety of conditions. Already at this stage one leaves the level where Piaget's epistemological analysis works, and turns to learning by prototype, now being explored by researchers such as Eleanor Rosch at Berkeley and Susan Block at M.I.T., whose work is casting doubt on the information-processing model assumed by Piaget.[13]

With experience, the chess beginner learns to recognize overextended positions and how to avoid them. Similarly, he begins to recognize such situational aspects of positions as a weakened king's side or a strong pawn structure despite the lack of precise and universally valid definitional rules.

STAGE 3: COMPETENCE

As experience increases, the number of features and aspects to be taken account of become overwhelming. To cope with this information explosion, the performer learns, or is taught, to adopt a hierarchical view of decision making. By first choosing a plan, goal, or perspective that organizes the situation and by then examining only the small set of features and aspects that he has learned are the most important given that plan, the performer can simplify and improve his performance.

Choosing a plan, a goal, or a perspective is no simple matter for the competent performer. It is not an objective procedure, like the feature recognition of the novice. Nor is the choice avoidable. While the advanced beginner can get along without recognizing and using a particular situational aspect until a sufficient number of examples makes identification easy and sure, to perform competently *requires* choosing an organizing goal or perspective. Furthermore, the choice of perspective crucially affects behavior in a way that one particular aspect rarely does.

This combination of necessity and uncertainty introduces an important new type of relationship between the performer and his environment. The novice and the advanced beginner applying rules and maxims feel little or no responsibility for the outcome of their acts. If they have made no mistakes, an unfortunate outcome is viewed as the result of inadequately specified elements or principles. The competent performer, on the other hand, after wrestling with the question of a choice of perspective or goal, feels responsible for and thus emotionally involved in the result of his choice. An outcome that is clearly successful is deeply satisfying and leaves a vivid memory of the situation encountered as seen from the goal or perspective finally chosen. Disasters, likewise, are not easily forgotten.

Remembered whole situations differ in one important respect from remembered aspects. The mental image of an aspect is flat in the sense that no parts stand out as salient. A whole situation, on the other hand, since it is the result of a chosen plan or perspective, has a three-dimensional quality. Certain elements stand out as more or less important with respect to the plan, while other irrelevant elements are forgotten. Moreover, the competent performer, gripped by the situation that his decision has produced, experiences and therefore remembers the situation not only in terms of foreground and background elements but also in terms of senses of opportunity, risk, expectations, threat, and so forth. These gripping, holistic memories cannot guide the behavior of the competent performer since he fails to make contact with them when he reflects on problematic situations as a detached observer, viewing himself as a computer following better and better rules. As we shall soon see, however, if he does let them take over, these memories become the basis of the competent performer's next advance in skill.

A competent driver beginning a trip decides, perhaps, that he is in a hurry. He then selects a route with attention to distance and time, ignores scenic beauty, and, as he drives, chooses his maneuvers with little concern for passenger comfort or for courtesy. He follows more closely than normal, enters traffic more daringly, occasionally violates a law. He feels elated when decisions work out and no police car appears, and shaken by near accidents and traffic tickets. (Beginners, on the other hand, can perpetrate chaos around them with total unconcern.)

The class-A chess player, here classed as competent, may decide after studying a position that his opponent has weakened his king's defenses so that an attack against the king is a viable goal. If the attack is chosen, features involving weaknesses in his own position created by his attack are ignored as are losses of pieces inessential to the attack. Removal of pieces defending the enemy king becomes salient. Successful plans induce euphoria and mistakes are felt in the pit of the stomach.

In both of these cases, we find a common pattern: detached planning, conscious assessment of elements that are salient with respect to the plan, and analytical rule-guided choice of action, followed by an emotionally involved experience of the outcome.

STAGE 4: PROFICIENCY

Considerable experience at the level of competency sets the stage for yet further skill enhancement. Having experienced many situations, chosen plans in each, and obtained vivid, involved demonstrations of the adequacy or inadequacy of the plan, the performer sees his current situation as similar to a previous one and so spontaneously sees an appropriate plan. Involved in the world of the skill, the performer "notices" or "is struck by" a certain plan, goal, or perspective. No longer is the spell of involvement broken by detached conscious planning.

There will, of course, be breakdowns of this "seeing," when, due perhaps to insufficient experience in a certain type of situation or to more than one possible plan presenting itself, the performer will need to take an analytical look at his situation. These are the sorts of situation studied by philosophers and cognitive psychologists. Between these breakdowns, however, the proficient performer will experience longer and longer intervals of continuous, intuitive understanding.

Since there are generally far fewer "ways of seeing" than "ways of acting," after understanding without conscious effort what is going on, the proficient performer will still have to think about what to do. During this thinking, elements that present themselves as salient are assessed and combined by rule and maxim to produce decisions about how best to manipulate the environment. The spell of involvement in the world of the activity will thus temporarily be broken.

On the basis of prior experience, a proficient driver approaching a curve on a rainy day may sense that he is traveling too fast. He then consciously determines an appropriate lower speed based on such salient elements as visibility, angle of road bank, criticality of time, and so forth. (These factors would be used by the *competent* driver consciously to *decide* that he is speeding.)

The proficient chess player, who is classed a master, can recognize a large repertoire of types of positions. Recognizing almost immediately and without conscious effort the sense of a position, he sets about calculating the move that best achieves his goal. He may, for example, know that he should attack, but he must deliberate about how best to do so.

STAGE 5: EXPERTISE

The proficient performer, immersed in the world of his skillful activity, *sees* what needs to be done, but *decides* how to do it. For the expert, not only situational understandings spring to mind, but also associated appropriate actions. The expert performer, except of course during moments of breakdown, understands, acts, and learns from results without any conscious awareness of the process. What transparently *must* be done *is* done. We usually do not make conscious, deliberative decisions when we walk, talk, ride a bicycle, drive, or carry on most social activities. An expert's skill has become so much a part of him that he need be no more aware of it than he is of his own body.

We have seen that experience-based similarity recognition produces the deep situational understanding of the proficient performer. No new insight is needed to explain the mental processes of the expert. With enough experience with a variety of situations, all seen from the same perspective or with the same goal in mind but requiring different tactical decisions, the mind of the proficient performer seems gradually to decompose this class of situations into subclasses, each member of which shares not only the same goal or perspective, but also the same decision, action, or tactic. At this point, not only is a situation, when seen as similar to members of this class, thereby understood but simultaneously the associated decision, action, or tactic presents itself.

The number of classes of recognizable situations, built up on the basis of experience, must be immense. It has been estimated that a master chess player can distinguish roughly 50,000 types of positions. Automobile driving probably involves a similar number of typical situations. We doubtless store far more typical situations in our memories than words in our vocabularies. Consequently, these reference situations, unlike the situational elements learned by the advanced beginner, bear no names and, in fact, defy complete verbal description.

The expert chess player, classed as an international master or grand master, in most situations experiences a compelling sense of the issue and the best move. Excellent chess players can play at the rate of 5–10 seconds a move and even faster without any serious degradation in performance. At this speed they must depend almost entirely on intuition and hardly at all on analyis and comparison of alternatives.

The expert driver, generally without any awareness, simply slows when his speed feels too fast until it feels right. He shifts gears when appropriate with no conscious awareness of his acts. Most drivers have experienced the disconcerting breakdown that occurs when suddenly one reflects on the gear-shifting process and tries to decide what to do. Suddenly the smooth, almost automatic, sequence of actions that results from the performer's involved immersion in the world of his skill is disrupted, and the performer sees himself, just as does the competent performer, as the manipulator of a complex mechanism. He detachedly calculates his actions even more poorly than does the competent performer, since he has forgotten many of the guiding rules and maxims that he knew and used when competent; his performance suddenly becomes halting, uncertain, and even inappropriate.

It seems that a beginner makes inferences using rules and facts just as a heuristically programmed computer does, but that with talent and a great deal of involved experience the beginner develops into an expert who intuitively sees what to do without applying rules. Of course, a description of skilled behavior can never be taken as conclusive evidence of what is going on in the mind or in the brain. It is always possible that what is going on is some unconscious process using more and more sophisticated rules. But our description of skill acquisition and successful skilled activity counters the traditional prejudice that expertise is analytic and procedural.

Until the traditional philosopher or epistemologist comes up with some argument or evidence that skills are implicit theories, educators would do well to side with the phenomena. If one does stick to the phenomena, one can understand why computer-assisted instruction (CAI) has worked well for drill but that when the tutor needs to understand the domain and the tutee, work so far has been disappointing. Moreover, the objection that the computer can be a dangerous tutee because analytical verbalized thinking is counterproductive gains new plausibility.

IMPLICATIONS OF OUR FIVE-STAGE MODEL OF SKILL ACQUISITION FOR CAI

The first concrete conclusion that follows from the above description is that, contrary to current opinion, there is nothing wrong with using computers for drill and practice. There is no reason to sneer when the computer is used as "a 'teaching' machine programmed to put children through their paces in arithmetic and spelling,"[14] or to think of the use of the computer for drill and practice, as Papert does, as an instance of the "qwerty" phenomenon—getting stuck like the typewriter keyboard in an early and inappropriate use of a new technology. Papert is right when he says:

> The idea of the computer as an instrument for drill and practice . . . appeals to teachers because it resembles traditional teaching methods [and] also appeals to the engineers who design computer systems. Drill and practice applications are predictable, simple to describe, efficient in use of the machine's resources. So the best engineering talent goes into the development of computer systems that are biased to favor this kind of application.[15]

But there is nothing sinister about these facts.

Papert is also correct, however, in stating that in domains that are rule-like, one can do better than to use the computer *merely* as drill sergeant. As our model of skill acquisition suggests, a beginner often needs to be given a rule or procedure, not just rote learning through repetition. In areas of simple computation such as subtraction there is no higher skill than the rapid and accurate application of appropriate rules. Yet even here Papert's view is one-sided. Computers can simply be given the right rule. After a student has become aware of the rule—perhaps by programming the computer to follow a certain procedure—he still has to have practice in applying the rule to various cases. So just as *drill* is appropriate for spelling where no rule can be trusted, *practice* is necessary for subjects like subtraction where rules are all there is. There is no reason to oppose drill and practice to learning by acquiring and debugging rules. Drill and practice are excellent ways to begin to acquire skills in appropriate domains. If computers can do either job faster and more painlessly than did older methods, more power to them.

But computers are so powerful and so logical, it seems there must be a way to use them beyond the drill-and-practice stage, to impart sophisticated understanding and higher levels of skill. It is this hope that makes both those who want to use the computer as tutor and those who want to use it as tutee condemn current software as inadequate and reactionary. Our five-stage model of skill acquisition enables us to better understand why progress to higher levels of skill acquisition has not taken place, and to cast a cold eye on such hopes.

The assumption behind CAI is that the success of drill programs should be extendable to areas in which what is required is not drill but understanding. It is generally agreed that this extension is not trivial. It requires giving the computer an understanding of the domain to be taught, an understanding of what the tutee already knows, and a representation of how the tutee is conceptualizing the problem. Otherwise the computer, like a talentless teacher, will painstakingly explain what the student already knows and take what is difficult as obvious, as well as failing to understand the student's difficulties. It is also generally agreed that so far computer tutors that go beyond drill and practice have been generally disappointing. At this point one usually hears or reads that more time and ingenuity will be required to produce better software. One finds no attempt to diagnose the difficulty.

One of the problems is that no one knows how to make a satisfactory model of a domain such as commonsense physics, so no one can put into a program the physical intuitions a physics tutor teaches. Likewise, and for exactly symmetrical reasons, no one is able to make a computer model of the everyday understanding the student brings to the learning task.

In the early seventies workers in AI had great success programming descriptions of what were called microworlds, very schematic descriptions of totally circumscribed domains. Papert called each microworld "a fairyland in which things are so simplified that almost every statement about them would be literally false if asserted about the real world."[16] But in the heyday of the success of such microworlds, AI workers expected that the techniques used in these schematic and isolated domains could be made gradually more realistic until they were able to describe the real world. This goal turned out to be unobtainable. In 1975, Patrick Winston, speaking for Papert, Minsky, and the AI Laboratory, concluded that "artificial intelligence has done well in tightly constrained domains. . . . Extending this kind of ability to larger worlds has not proved straightforward, however. . . . The time has come to treat the problems involved as central issues."[17] Now, the difficulties are being faced. As Roger Schank of Yale recently remarked: "Researchers are starting to understand that tour-de-forces in programming are interesting but non-extendable . . . the AI people recognize that how people use and represent knowledge is the key issue in the field."[18]

Papert and Minsky give an excellent example of the sort of difficulties involved in representing even the commonsense knowledge involved in a relatively restricted domain such as our everyday knowledge of physical reality (which makes no reference to human beings, culture, etc.):

> Many problems arise in experiments on machine intelligence because things obvious to any person are not represented in any programs. One can pull with a string, but one cannot push with one. One cannot push with a thin wire, either. A taut inextensible cord will break under a very small lateral force. Pushing something affects first its speed; only indirectly its position! Simple facts like these . . . have not been faced up to until now.[19]

And now, even though they have been faced up to, no one in AI has a clue how to deal with them. Spelling out a tutor's understanding of the physical world—an understanding that is partly conceptual and partly embodied in his or her mastery of skills for coping with physical things—would seem a hopeless task given the years of experience that have gone into the teacher's understanding of the field, not to mention the time a child takes in the sensory-motor stage developing an intuitive feel for solids and liquids, and so forth. But the Socratic assumption is invoked, usually as self-evident, to save AI and CAI researchers from despair. After all, if the child can come to understand commonsense physics, one ought to be able to get at the facts the child knows and the rules he uses to relate them, and so make a model of the child's knowledge—which, of course, could then be updated with more and more sophisticated rules as the child learns to debug his earlier hypotheses. Likewise, the physics teacher, if he already understands physics, must already have a program for that domain, which we simply have to extract and put into the teaching system.

Of course, this will be hard. As Minsky noted ten years ago:

> Just constructing a knowledge base is a major intellectual research problem. . . . We still know far too little about the contents and structure of common-sense knowledge. A "minimal" common-sense system must "know" something about cause-effect, time, purpose, locality, process, and types of knowledge. . . . We need a serious epistemological research effort in this area.[20]

But philosophers from Plato to Piaget, who uncovered all these problems and more, have carried on serious epistemological research in this area for two thousand years without notable success. This, plus the fact that no significant progress in AI has been reported since the commonsense knowledge problem surfaced a decade ago, suggests that there is a limit to how far one can go with a rule-and-feature model of knowledge.

Our model of skill acquisition predicts and explains this impasse. If our experience of skill acquisition is to be trusted, and we have nothing else to trust, our everyday expertise is not "stored" in the mind in terms of facts and rules at all, but in our memories of past situations already successfully confronted. If the knowledge to be represented is the knowledge of an expert rather than that of a beginner, aspects, saliency, and finally the memory of whole patterns have to be introduced into the program. Unfortunately, these functions cannot be simulated on a heuristically programmed digital computer. Computers do not store images or any picture-like representations of objects and situations. They can store only descriptions. Thinkers who accept the information-processing paradigm tend to blur this distinction. Thus Papert often speaks of the advantage of LOGO as making the formalism of mathematics concrete: "The computer can concretize (and personalize) the formal."[21] But the computer does not allow the storage of specific situations in total detail with the concreteness of an image. All a program can do is to substitute one set of abstractions and formal descriptions for another. The ability of computers to store and manipulate symbolic descriptions and thousands of rules with great accuracy and speed makes them at best "expert novices." They are, however, able to store neither the sort of prototypes necessary for recognizing the aspects recognized by an advanced beginner, nor the whole patterns necessary for expertise.

Likewise, since no two concrete situations will ever be identical, the use of aspects and of whole situations requires that the current scene be recognized as *similar* to one already experienced. Computers, however, cannot recognize similarity without analyzing it into identity of components. Thus, Herbert Simon, who recognizes that chess players see perhaps 50,000 patterns, thinks of these patterns as specific components of a whole position, such as knight forks, passed pawns, pinned knights, and so forth, which can be recognized as identical from situation to situation. This is the best a computer can do, but programs based on such analysis do not exhibit expertise.

In the light of these intrinsic limitations on computers and so on the information-processing model of the mind, we can now understand why one cannot program the understanding the tutor and the student bring to a subject such as physics. These limitations do not show the need for more ideas and more sophisticated programs; rather they reveal the limits on what one can expect from computer-aided instruction. The computer can be used as tutor, all right, but only for drill and practice. Instead of entertaining vain hopes of higher intelligence, one should appreciate and utilize the computer's capacity for tireless, accurate, attractive drill, with instant feedback and up-to-date records.

The real danger of CAI is not that our children will become programmed as in *1984,* as Papert prophesied on a recent "Nova" program. The real danger is perseveration in the use of the inadequate tutorial programs on the market, rather than admitting that the beginning student can use rules only up to a point, after which he must be allowed to pass beyond analysis to higher stages of skill acquisition, where human tutors can point out prototypes and where apprenticeship and practice alone can produce expertise.

IMPLICATIONS FOR USING THE COMPUTER AS TUTEE

The limitations of the computer as tutor lead Papert to propose using the computer as tutee. Our model of skill acquisition enables us to see why Papert's ideas are so persuasive and work so well, and also enables us to warn against a danger that Papert's commitment to the information-processing model of the mind leads him to overlook.

Papert has the wisdom to see that any attempt to use the computer in education must be based on a theory of how the mind works and specifically of how learning takes place. He is one of the few thinkers in the field to have worked out an explicit theory, which he applies consistently in his work and writing. The theory, which, following Piaget, he calls "epistemological," is that the mind works like a computer. The resulting model of the mind as an information processing mechanism is often called "cognitivism." The microcomputer reinforces the attraction of the cognitivist's model of thinking, and Papert's brilliant insight is that children can master this way of thinking by actually programming the computer, which, since it can deal only with data and rules, is an epistemological engine par excellence. Programming the computer requires the child to articulate his own program by reflecting on and naming the features he is picking out in his environment and by making explicit the procedures he is using to relate these features to events in the learning domain. Papert says:

> I have invented ways to take educational advantage of the opportunities to master the art of *deliberately* thinking like a computer, according, for example, to the stereotype of a computer program that proceeds in a step-by-step, literal, mechanical fashion. . . . What is most important in this is that through these experiences these children would be serving their apprenticeships as epistemologists, that is to say learning to think articulately about thinking.[22]

Papert is aware that there are those who object to this approach.

> Some people say: we know very little about cognitive psychology; we surely do not want to teach such half-baked theories in our school! And some people say: making the children self-conscious about learning will surely impede their learning. Asked for evidence they usually tell stories like the one about a millipede who was asked which foot he moved first when he walked. Apparently the attempt to verbalize the previously unconscious action prevented the poor beast from ever walking again.[23]

But he considers these objections flimsy. He answers that the child will in any case form some view of how the mind works, so we had better give him the best one available: "The real choice is: *either* give the child the best ideas we can muster about cognitive processes *or* leave him at the mercy of the theories he invents or picks up in the gutter. The question is: who can do better, the child or us?"[24]

Papert is dramatic and convincing when he points out the revolutionary effect that giving the child an explicit grasp of the cognitivist approach to the mind would have on education.

> We are at a point in the history of education when radical change is possible, and the possibility for that change is directly tied to the impact of the computer. Today what is offered in the education "market" is largely determined by what is acceptable to a sluggish and conservative system. But this is where the computer presence is in the process of creating an environment for change.[25]

And, like a true revolutionary, he sees that actually implementing his cognitivist ideas would transform our understanding of ourselves and of our whole society.

> In a computer-rich world, computer languages that simultaneously provide a means of control over the computer and offer new and powerful descriptive languages for thinking will undoubtedly be carried into the general culture. They will have a particular effect on our language for describing ourselves and our learning.[26]

The stakes are high. It is very important, then, before embarking on Papert's educational reform to look at both the power and the limitations of his cognitivist view of education and of ourselves. If our critique is to be constructive and sound, rather than conservative and flimsy, it will have to be based on a model of the mind that points up the cognitivist's insights, as well as their systematic oversights. Our five-stage model of skill acquisition provides just the framework we need.

To begin with, we can understand why anyone beginning to acquire a skill in a new domain needs to learn to recognize basic features and rules or procedures for combining them, and to act on them. So, for example, for learning addition algorithms, Papert's model works perfectly: "Learning algorithms can be seen as a process of making, using, and fixing programs. When one adds multidigit numbers one is in fact acting as a computer."[27] Here any aid such as being able to name the elements and verbalize the procedures might well be a great help, so we can agree with Papert that

> a fundamental problem for the theory of mathematical education is to identify and name the concepts needed to enable the beginner to discuss his mathematical thinking in a clear articulate way. And when we know such concepts we may want to seek out (or invent!) areas of mathematical work which exemplify these concepts particularly well.[28]

It also seems reasonable that putting the child in the role of tutor to the computer should accelerate the acquisition of this understanding.

Another useful concept at this beginning stage is the notion of microworld: "The use of the micro-worlds provides a model of a learning theory in which active learning consists of exploration by the learner of a micro-world sufficiently bounded and transparent for constructive exploration and yet sufficiently rich for significant discovery."[29]

The fact that the microworld failed as a step toward modeling real-world understanding does not prevent it from being recuperated as a simplified environment, in which the beginner can more easily pick out the features he needs to recognize, and in which the procedures he is learning apply automatically.

There are also further advantages in getting the child to think about his own thinking on the model of the computer. As Papert points out:

> Trouble with adding is not seen as symptomatic of something else; it is trouble with the *procedure* of adding. For the computerist the procedure

> and the ways it can go wrong are fully as interesting and as conceptual as anything else. Moreover, *what* went wrong, namely the bugs, are not seen as mistakes to be avoided like the plague, but as an intrinsic part of the learning process.[30]

Finally, writing a program to perform the task is a long-range project that can engage the student's interest and so promote involvement in a way that solving isolated problems cannot.

> A child interested in flying model airplanes under computer control will work at this project over a long period. He will have time to try different approaches to sub-problems. He will have time to talk about it, to establish a common language with a collaborator or an instructor, to relate it to other interests and problems. This *project-oriented* approach contrasts with the *problem* approach of most math teaching: a bad feature of the typical problem is that the child does not stay with it long enough to benefit much from success or from failure.
>
> Along with time scale goes structure. A project is long enough to have recognizable phases—such as planning, choosing a strategy of attempting a very simple case first, finding the simple solution, *debugging it*, and so on. And if the time scale is long enough, and the structures clear enough, the child can develop a vocabulary for articulate discussion of the process of working towards his goals.[31]

All this is very persuasive. Still, one must remain critical. As we mentioned earlier in discussing subtraction rules, one must have practice in applying these rules. Since a computer gets the rules at one fell swoop, and since they apply automatically in the microworld, where there are no exceptions and no ambiguity, Papert underestimates the need for practice, and the changes that go with experience. He neglects the fact that with enough practice the beginner will be ready to notice aspects, and to use maxims that apply to them.

At this advanced-beginner stage the microworld idea can actually get in the way of learning. If what the learner were acquiring were more and more sophisticated features and rules, then one could neglect aspects and gradually complicate the microworlds as the child developed greater skill. But if, as our skill model suggests, the learner is acquiring a repertory of aspects and of whole, real-world situations, then keeping the learner in a microworld can actually be counterproductive. It might help a beginner learn some basic ideas of chess if one simplified the rules, by, for example, making all exchanges forced as in checkers. One could still pick out and name features like center control and knight forks, and even some aspects like unbalanced pawn structure, but in playing such games over and over one would not be acquiring a stock of prototypical *whole* situations with their associated successful response. Or, to take our other example, driving in a parking lot might help a beginning driver to learn to shift, but finally no simplified microworld can substitute for driving on roads with other cars and pedestrians all around, since it is memories of such concrete situations that are required for expertise.

Although the microworld approach may well be a dead end even for advanced beginners, the idea of the student as tutor can still be helpful. Since the student needs to learn to recognize aspects, the student might well be led to find these aspects by acting as teacher or coach. Still, it is important to realize that one can name aspects and recite maxims, but one cannot *program* them. As we saw in discussing the world of the advanced beginner, aspects like engine sound and unbalanced pawn structure can be recognized by similarity to prototypes but not decomposed into the sort of objective features required by a computer program.

Just as in the case of an advanced beginner, when passing on to competence there is still some use for analysis and verbalization. One can learn the names of specific strategies and the features and aspects that suggest which strategy to apply. Using programming as a metaphor might help develop this analytic planning capacity.

Papert speaks convincingly of this pedagogical use of the computer model, and defends its generalization.

> I believe in articulate discussion (in monologue or dialogue) of how one solves problems, of why one goofed that one, of what gaps or deformations exist in one's knowledge and of what could be done about it. I shall defend this belief against two quite distinct objections. One objection says: "*it's impossible to verbalize*; problems are solved by intuitive acts of insight and these cannot be articulated." The other objection says: "*it's bad to verbalize*; remember the centipede who was paralyzed when the toad asked which leg came after which."[32]

But Papert's defenses are flimsy, to adopt his favorite pejorative. At the next stage, proficiency, where the learner must see whole patterns and remember them, analysis no longer helps; it actually gets in the way. One *could* name issues and whole patterns. There is nothing mystical or ineffable about them. But since there are probably more subtly differentiated patterns in the mind of the chess grand master than we have words in our whole vocabulary, pointing them out and naming them is a hopeless task. More important, since pattern storage and retrieval takes place without conscious awareness, there is no point in having names for the patterns learned. To see this point it helps to remember that in linguistics we have a huge vocabulary for describing grammar, tense, aspect, conjugation, declension, and so forth, and that being able to pick out such features and rules does seem to help a beginner learn a second language. For such a beginner it might well be helpful, as Papert suggests at one point, to try to program a computer to produce sentences in a simplified grammar of the language being learned. But as anyone who has learned a foreign language knows, such knowledge of vocabulary and rules does not create proficiency. One needs experience speaking, reading, and listening. Then one can finally stop thinking of rules and speak flexibly and fluently—even sometimes breaking the rules—in a wide variety of situations.

This example serves to illustrate an important point. While thinking of oneself as a computer acquiring features and procedures might well accelerate the passage from beginner to advanced-beginner stage, and can still be a useful metaphor in passing from advanced beginner to competence, it follows from our model of skill acquisition that thinking like a computer will retard passage to proficiency and expertise.

CONCLUSION

Before drawing the moral of the above discussion, it is important to separate the issue raised by Papert's proposal that children should become epistemologists—that is, should come to think of themselves as employing procedures in solving problems—and the related issue of whether such procedures do in fact underlie expertise. The former is a question that must be asked if one is to have a view of the proper role of computers in education; the second concerns the truth of cognitive psychology, but need not concern the educator. For education the crucial question is not whether skills are implicit theories, as Leibniz, Piaget, Polanyi, and Papert think, but whether it facilitates learning to get the student to think of skills in this way.

Our contention is that whether there is a tacit theory underlying expertise or not, it is counterproductive to base an educational program on such an idea. We will argue first, against the computer as tutor, that at the higher stages of skill acquisition, even if there are rules underlying expertise, the rules that the expert has access to are not the rules that generate his expertise, and so learning them will not improve performance, and, second, against the computer as tutee, that trying to find rules or procedures in a domain often stands in the way of learning even at the earliest stages. True to our conviction that an example equals a thousand inferences, we will use two illustrations that can be taken as parables, to make these two points.

In the Air Force, instructor pilots teach beginning pilots, among other things, how to scan their instruments. The instructor pilots teach the beginning pilots the rule for instrument scanning that they, the instructor pilots, were taught, and, as far as they know, still use. At one point, however, Air Force psychologists studied the eye movement of the instructors as they actually flew and found, to everyone's surprise, that the instructor pilots were not following the rule they were teaching.[33] In fact, as far as the psychologists could determine, they were not following any rule at all. If one accepts our five-stage model of skill acquisition, this should be no surprise. The instructors, after years of experience, had learned to scan the instruments in flexible and situationally appropriate ways.

Now suppose that the instructor pilots give their account of what they know and teach to a team of CAI specialists and that these specialists put this "knowledge" into a CAI system. The computer tutor now begins, like the instructor pilots, by drilling the beginners in applying the rule. Moreover, the computer tests the beginners by asking them questions and following their eye movements to be sure that they have learned the rule and are applying it correctly. So far so good. But later, after much experience, the beginner will be ready to make the leap to situational understanding, achieving proficiency by leaving behind any awareness of rules and responding immediately to similarity to specific previous situations—the same move the instructor pilots made without realizing it. At this point, since recognition of similarity to a previous situation is not the sort of tacit knowledge that can be made explicit as rules, and no one has access to any other rules, there is nothing more for the computer tutor to teach. The proficient performer is on his own.

If, however, one insists on generalizing the CAI method and its success in teaching beginners to higher levels of skill acquisition, we then get an educational horror story. The computer tutor, like the sorcerer's apprentice, continues to check the protocols and eye movements of the student pilot and forces him to return to the rule whenever he starts to violate it. Or, in a slightly more elaborate nightmare, the computer has been programmed with more and more sophisticated rules for the student to learn. In either case, the student is prevented by the accuracy, relentlessness, and record-keeping powers of the computer tutor from making the transition from rule-following, analytic competence to intuitive proficiency and expertise. This is clearly a disastrous educational practice, even in the unlikely case that it turns out that cognitivism is correct and that experts follow unconscious and inaccessible programs.

In most domains, then, expertise is possible only if the tutor can allow the student to quiet the analytical mind and act intuitively, whether the brain is a computer with a program or not. In other domains, one cannot even begin to learn if one thinks of oneself as an information processor and tries to program the computer as tutee by extracting a rule that describes the structure of the domain. In such a domain, to approach the learning task as if one were a programmer trying to extract a program makes learning impossible.

This is no "flimsy" humanitarian objection, but the conclusion of psychological experiments performed by Lee Brooks and published in an important article, "Nonanalytic Concept Formation and Memory for Instances."[34] Brooks constructed two complicated artificial grammars and used a computer to construct strings of letters that followed the grammatical rules and other strings that did not. He then divided his subjects into two groups. The first was shown a set of strings generated by grammar A and another set generated by grammar B. They were given the task of abstracting the two sets of rules from the two sets of examples. The second group of subjects was given the same two sets of examples, but told nothing of the rules. Rather, one set of strings of letters was paired with the names of cities and the other was paired with names of animals. These subjects were told to memorize the pairs. They had no idea that the experiment involved concept learning. Each set of subjects was given the same amount of time to perform the learning task. The first group tried to find the rules defining which strings fell into which grammatical category; the second group tried to remember which string of letters was paired with which animal or city.

Each group was then tested to see what it had learned. The first group had learned nothing since they were unable to abstract the arbitrary and complex rules used in generating the grammatical strings. What was surprising was what happened in the second group. Unknown to them, the strings had been arranged so that strings from grammar A were paired with Old-World cities and animals, while strings from grammar B were paired with New-World items. When they were presented with thirty new cases Brooks recounts the astonishing results:

> The subjects were told that 10 of these cards contained a new string of letters that should be the name of an Old-World item, 10 that should be the name of a New-World item, and 10 that did not belong to either category. Their job was to sort them into these three categories. Their initial response was . . . giggles or irritation together with an emphatic protestation that they didn't know what they were doing. . . . [Yet] they were able to distinguish each of the three categories from one another at a level well above chance.[35]

Brooks concludes that in "the contrast between deliberate, verbal, analytic control processes and implicit, intuitive, nonanalytic processes . . . too loose a use of the word 'rule' has served to submerge the likely fact that much of our knowledge is a loose confederation of special cases in which our knowledge of the general is often overridden by our knowledge of the particular. . . . Stressing the nonanalytic, instance-oriented strategy could . . . under some circumstances allow the learner to deal with more complicated problems than would an analytic strategy."[36]

The moral for the use of the computer as tutee is obvious. Whatever the unconscious was doing—whether the brain was abstracting rules or not—thinking of oneself as a computer and therefore looking for rules prevented the brain from doing its job, and stood in the way of learning. In some domains at least, if one starts with the analytical approach one must be especially careful *not* to think of oneself as a computer and *not* to think of learning as finding procedures, or one can not even begin. It is ironic to find Papert agreeing with Timothy Gallwey of *Inner Tennis* fame, who is the most articulate defender of this point.

> Gallwey encourages the learner to think of himself as made up of two selves: an analytic, verbal self and a more holistic, intuitive one. It is

> appropriate, he argues, that now one and now the other of these two selves should be in control; in fact, an important part of the learning process is teaching each "self" to know when to take over and when to leave it to the other. . . . Gallwey's strategy is to help learners learn how to make the choice for themselves, a perspective that is in line with the vision already suggested of the child as epistemologist, where the child is encouraged to become expert in recognizing and choosing among varying styles of thought.[37]

Papert implies that one can use either the analytical or intuitive approach at all levels of learning, whereas Gallwey's whole method consists in helping the learner achieve mastery by preventing analytical thinking from the very start. It is simply not true that Gallwey has achieved his great success in teaching skills by suggesting that sometimes the analytic, verbal self and sometimes the holistic, intuitive self should be in control, and that the learner should choose among these various styles of thought. *Our* model does suggest that, sometimes at least, the beginner should be encouraged to think like an epistemologist, but Gallwey's whole strategy consists of avoiding the trap of getting stuck in rational procedures, passing directly to proficient performance by totally bypassing the analytical mind.

Papert and Gallwey represent two extreme approaches to skill acquisition. Papert tries to create a learning environment in which the learner is constantly faced with new problems and needs to discover new rules; he treats the learner as a perpetual beginner. Gallwey, on the other hand, would like to create a learning environment in which there were no problems at all so that there was never any need for analytical reflection. Our view is that at any stage of learning problems arise that require rational, analytical thought, and the learner must learn how to think them through. That is the value of Papert's computer model. Nonetheless, skill in a domain is measured by the performer's ability to act appropriately in situations that might once have been problems but no longer require analytical reflection. The risk of Gallwey's method is that it leaves the expert without the tools to solve new problems, but the risk of Papert's approach is far greater. It would leave the learner a perpetual beginner, by encouraging the dependence on rules that blocks the acquisition of expertise.

We have seen that Taylor and the authors he anthologizes think, like Socrates and Plato, that we cannot teach what we do not understand and that we understand only what we can formulate in the sort of rules and procedures used by a computer. If this were true, teachers could be gradually replaced by computers. But teachers are no doubt aware that their own expertise in teaching does not consist in knowing complicated *rules* about coaching—what tips to give, when to keep silent and when to intervene—although they may have learned such rules in graduate school. What an expert teacher gains from experience is not more rules of coaching of the sort they once explicitly followed as beginners. Rather, the teacher learns intuitively and spontaneously to provide the tips and examples needed by the advanced beginner, and to motivate the involved practice by which a student gains proficiency in any domain.

Even Socrates, who was trying to spell out his understanding in explicit rules and objected to Euthyphro's concrete examples, is not remembered as a great teacher because of the heuristics he dragged out of people's unconscious. Indeed, Socrates knew that by his rational standards he knew nothing; in his whole life he had not dredged up and debugged a single heuristic rule. What made Socrates a great teacher was what he *did* rather than what he *knew*. His life became an exemplar that many have sought to imitate precisely because, as he says in the *Apology*, his life and death were directed by an intuition and commitment he could neither explicate nor elude.

Notes

1 The issues raised in this article will be treated in greater detail in Hubert L. Dreyfus and Stuart E. Dreyfus, *Putting Computers in Their Place* (New York: William Morrow, forthcoming).

2 See Hubert L. Dreyfus, *What Computers Can't Do* (New York: Harper & Row, 1979).

3 Robert Taylor, ed., *The Computer in the School: Tutor, Tool, Tutee* (New York: Teachers College Press, 1980), p. 1.

4 Plato, *Euthyphro*, trans. F. J. Church (New York: Liberal Arts Press, 1948), p. 7.

5 Thomas Hobbes, *Leviathan* (New York: Liberal Arts Press, 1958), p. 45.

6 Leibniz, *Selections*, ed. Philip Wiener (New York: Charles Scribner's Sons, 1951), p. 48. Italics added.

7 George Boole, *Laws of Thought*, Collected Logical Works, Vol. II (La Salle, Ill.: Open Court, 1940), p. 1.

8 Taylor, *The Computer in the School*, p. 4.

9 Seymour Papert, *Mindstorms: Children, Computers, and Powerful Ideas* (New York: Harper & Row, 1980), p. 96.

10 Ibid., p. 28.

11 Ibid., p. 113.

12 Patricia Benner, "From Novice to Expert," *American Journal of Nursing* 82, no. 3 (March 1982): 402-07.

13 Susan Carey Block, *Conceptual Change in Childhood* (Cambridge: M.I.T. Press, forthcoming).

14 Papert, *Mindstorms*, p. 29.

15 Ibid., p. 36.

16 Marvin Minsky and Seymour Papert, Draft, July 1970, of a Proposal to ARPA for Research on Artificial Intelligence at M.I.T., 1970-1971, p. 39.

17 Patrick H. Winston and the Staff of the M.I.T. AI Laboratory, AI Memo. No. 366 (May 1976), p. 22.

18 Roger C. Schank et al., Panel on Natural Language Processing (IJCAI-77, Proceedings), pp. 107 and 108.

19 M.I.T. AI Laboratory, Memo. No. 299 (September 1973), p. 77.

20 Marvin Minsky, unpublished draft of the frame paper, February 27, 1974, p. 68. Printed in *Mind Design*, ed. John Haugeland (Cambridge: Bradford/M.I.T. Press, 1981).

21 Papert, *Mindstorms*, p. 21.

22 Ibid., p. 27.

23 Seymour Papert, "Teaching Children Thinking," in Taylor, *The Computer in the School*, p. 163.

24 Ibid.

25 Papert, *Mindstorms*, pp. 36-37.

26 Ibid., p. 98.

27 Ibid., p. 152.

28 Seymour Papert, "Teaching Children to be Mathematicians," in Taylor, *The Computer in the School*, p. 180.

29 Taylor, *The Computer in the School*, p. 208.

30 Papert, *Mindstorms*, p. 153.

31 Papert, "Teaching Children to be Mathematicians," pp. 179-80.

32 Ibid., p. 180.

33 J. DeMaio et al., "Visual Scanning: Comparisons between Student and Instructor Pilots," AFHRL-TR-76-10, AD-A023 634 (Williams AFB, Ariz.: Flying Training Division, Air Force Human Resources Laboratory, June 1976).

34 Lee Brooks, "Nonanalytic Concept Formation and Memory for Instances," in *Cognition and Categorization*, ed. Eleanor Rosch and Barbara Lloyd (Hillsdale, N.J.: Lawrence Erlbaum Associates, 1978.

35 Ibid., pp. 172-73.

36 Ibid., pp. 207-09.

37 Papert, *Mindstorms*, pp. 97-98.

Computer Literacy and Ideology

DOUGLAS NOBLE
Rochester, New York

The need for some form of "computer literacy" has come to be accepted as an essential condition of everyday life, now that the computer has insinuated itself into our jobs, our schools, and our homes. As a result, computer-literacy education has become very big business, evidenced by the myriad of computer classes, workshops, and camps available to people of all ages. The purpose of all this training, we are told, is not to make engineers or programmers of everyone; rather, its focus is on a minimal level of instruction that will introduce the masses to the ubiquitous computer and enable them to feel "comfortable," to have "a sense of belonging in a computer-rich society."[1]

Although this goal seems reasonably straightforward, its promoters, while insisting on the critical importance of computer literacy, have had unusual difficulty arriving at a suitable definition. "No one can tell you exactly what it is," writes one promoter, "but everyone is sure that it is good for us."[2] This unexamined conviction, more felt than understood, has somehow triggered a mass educational campaign whose urgent, uncritical endorsement is without precedent in the history of technological education.

This article is in two parts. The first part will show that computer literacy, however it may be defined, is unimportant, despite its plausibility and its fervent promotion. The second part will attempt to explain the enormous appeal of computer literacy despite its unimportance. It will be suggested that the computer-literacy phenomenon might best be viewed not as education, but rather as an ideological campaign, one that coincides with and reinforces a hegemonic vision of a computerized future.

COMPUTER LITERACY FOR AN INFORMATION AGE: MYTH VERSUS REALITY

Arguments that have been used to justify the importance of computer literacy can be reduced to four, each corresponding to a role of daily life in the "information age":

1. Consumers must be computer literate in order to function in the computerized marketplace.

The author wishes to thank Philip Wexler, Lynne Kliman, David Noble, Martha Herrick, and Molly Pierce for their ideas and assistance.

2. Students must be computer literate in order to cope with the computerized "learning revolution" in schools and colleges.
3. Workers must be computer literate in order to survive in the "high-technology" work force.
4. Citizens must be computer literate in order to vote and take an active part in the "information society."

CONSUMER LITERACY

Turning first to the needs of the consumer, we find that while computers are indeed invading the marketplace and the home, there is nothing one has to know about computers in order to function successfully in a world of electronic ovens, "moneymatic" machines, and multifunction watches. "The future," according to one manufacturer, "lies in designing and selling computers that people don't realize are computers at all."[3] Although there may be as many home computers as television sets by the year 2000,[4] this will happen only as they become as easily accessible. Even today the majority of home computers are used exclusively for packaged games;[5] most other home uses, such as budgeting or filing recipes, require little more than inserting a cartridge or disk and following simple directions on a screen.

How then are we to understand the consumer's supposed need to be computer literate? It is of course true that computer enthusiasts need to know how to program and how to find their way through a maze of computer products, but most consumers are not in this category. To purchase or to repair computer products one will be able to turn to knowledgeable friends, salesmen, or technicians, just as consumers today do with their cars and television sets. Although it might be nice to be able to do it all oneself, such dependence in the world of cars and television sets is hardly seen as dysfunctional today, and so it will be with computers tomorrow. In fact, as computers become more standardized, more self-diagnostic, more "user-friendly," such dependence will be far less problematic than that of today's typical car owner.

It is often said that "using computers is going to be just like driving a car,"[6] but given the ease with which a typical teenager learns how to drive, it is difficult to understand why this analogy is offered as an argument for computer literacy. Furthermore, such a skill as driving is best acquired as the need for it arises; similarly, people can learn whatever they need or want to know about computers without having to be prepared or "literate" beforehand. The idea of computer literacy as preparation for later application, seen, for example, in comparisons between computer literacy and music appreciation, fits nicely within a "basic-skill" mentality that refuses to allow that fundamental knowledge is best acquired in the process of useful activity, not beforehand in useless introduction.

STUDENT LITERACY

What about the vision of a computer revolution in the schools? Although there is a host of new computer requirements, the schools offer a world of shortsighted goals, exaggerated promise, and premature pronouncements, typically in response to intense outside pressures. Despite anecdotes of success, recent observers find computers in education to be at "a stage no more advanced than Kitty Hawk,"[7] with equipment still spread so thinly as to be "considerably less than a revolution."[8] Added to these limitations are the enormous problems of untrained teachers, inadequate courseware, insufficient funds, and the wide disparity of access between rich and poor school districts. Yet promoters of computer literacy still talk of a total transformation of education for which all students must be prepared.

Computers will be useful, they tell us, both as powerful instructional aids and as catalysts for creative thinking and problem solving. Neither of these uses, however, appears to warrant the urgent, immediate attention it is receiving. Computer-assisted instruction ranges from sophisticated simulations to drill and practice. Computer simulation courseware, although exciting in concept, is still largely experimental, limited, and untested. Drill-and-practice programs, often poorly developed and thoughtlessly utilized, are most effective in catching the attention of just those disadvantaged students whose access to them is the most limited. Even where available, their long-term benefits are unexamined and doubtful, given the complexity of such students' educational problems.

In addition to computer-assisted instruction, computers in schools are said to offer new opportunities for problem solving and intellectual development, and programming languages such as LOGO are touted as capable of bringing difficult ideas within the reach of young children.[9] Despite considerable excitement, however, this work is still in its infancy and "there is little objective data confirming the contention that computer programming enhances intellectual functioning or problem-solving."[10] The truth is that "current research has only begun to scratch the surface in exploring whether what students learn by programming computers has any carryover into non-computer situations."[11] Intuitions aside, programming remains for now an end in itself, often fun and stimulating, just as often misapplied or purposeless. In any case it is hardly worth the fuss.

Given the present state of computers in education, a reasonable agenda for the schools might include funds for promising computer projects, student exposure to computers along with woodshop or cooking, a social studies focus on the idea of technological progress, and programming courses for interested students. Promoters of computer literacy, however, see things on a grander scale. Portraying themselves as pioneers on a new frontier, they translate deficiencies into challenges and call for massive support to intensify and broaden their efforts to use the computer to transform education.

Meanwhile, "computer science" has suddenly become a "New Basic" in the recommendations of the Presidental Commission on Excellence in Education,[12] despite the fact that it will meet no fundamental need of students in the years to come.

WORKER LITERACY

Computer literacy might be unnecessary to students while they are in school, but it is widely believed that "computer training should be . . . basic in schools [in order to] achieve a level of literacy that workers will need to get good jobs in the years ahead."[13] Indeed, since computers are thought to be transforming the very nature of work in the information age, computer literacy is being urged as necessary for employment in general.

Recent studies using Bureau of Labor Statistics data, however, challenge these assumptions by showing that very few of tomorrow's jobs will require any familiarity with computers.[14] While millions of workers are being permanently replaced by computers and robotics, new job areas created by computer technology—those that are not exported—are typically capital-intensive, creating relatively few new jobs. Despite prevailing assumptions, only 7 percent of the new work force will involve high-tech positions for programmers, technicians, computer operators, and engineers, and any current shortages in these areas will soon be filled.[15] Most job openings in the next decade will be for janitors, nurses' aides, sales clerks, kitchen helpers, and truck drivers. None of these jobs requires any familiarity with computers, however much they might depend upon computers behind the scenes. In addition, the vast majority of workers who will need to know something about computers, such as travel agents, airline reservationists, or telephone operators, will be able to learn what they need to know about their particular machines in a few weeks or less. In fact, the computer industry itself has begun to question its own workers' need for computer literacy, which, it says, can be developed on the job.[16]

Why then is computer literacy considered so important for employment? One answer is that computer literacy represents high tech and the assumption is made that jobs in any age of high technology will require high-technology skills. Historically, however, the "higher" the technology introduced into a job, the lower the skills required by that job become. In numerical control machining, checkout scanning, or word processing, for example, most of the competence is built directly into the machines themselves. Smarter machines require less-skilled workers.

A second answer involves the assumption that any job touched by the computer is thereby transformed into "mind work" or "knowledge work" typical of tomorrow's jobs. According to this view, "future workers will need the conceptual basis for solving complex problems and handling large systems of information."[17] Once again, the opposite is closer to the truth:

Those jobs affected by computers, even attractive jobs like programming,[18] are being subjected to new, tighter forms of control and segmentation that transform them into what might be more appropriately called "mindless work."

Computer literacy does not prepare people for potent, intellectual work, but even if it did, such work will be rare in tomorrow's labor market. There is instead every indication that computers will be used to preserve existing relations of knowledge and power on the job rather than to disturb them, and that there will still be little room at the top.

Of course, corporate managers, small businessmen, and professionals will probably need to know something about computers to perform their transformed tasks, but these people usually learn specific packages on particular machines as the need arises. General computer literacy is almost worthless in this context and will be even less useful as computer systems become more user-friendly (in fact rather than promise) in the wake of Apple's Lisa, which is claimed to reduce instructional time from forty hours to forty minutes.[19] The need for computer literacy is therefore questionable even for the few attractive jobs in tomorrow's work force; for everyone else, it is unquestionably a waste of time.

CITIZEN LITERACY

What about the argument that computer literacy is necessary for citizenship? Will tomorrow's citizen need to know something about computers in order to make informed decisions in the information age? One reads that "some understanding of computer programming is necessary for the exercise of the rights and responsibilities of citizenship."[20] But this claim is difficult to understand, given the emphasis in computer-literacy education on trivial technical competence. Even if expertise in computers were necessary for informed policy decisions about their design or use, the level of technical knowledge offered in computer literacy classes is many orders of magnitude removed from the understanding of large systems that could conceivably contribute to public deliberation.

Technical understanding or expertise, however, is not necessary for participation in the social control of computer technology. Instead, one needs political understanding and a knowledge of who controls the direction of computer policy, for what purposes, for whose benefit, and for whose loss. There is nothing in computer-literacy education that offers such information or insight. Instead, discussions of "social" questions are typically underplayed and oversimplified, serving as testimonials to such wonders as the automated office, the unmanned factory, and the Star Wars arsenal. The uncritical manner in which these topics are typically taught, especially in teacher-training workshops, reduces the dissemination of computer literacy to instances of the blind leading the blind on matters of social importance.

Still we are told that "to function effectively as citizens, we will need to know how the computer impinges on and enhances our everyday lives."[21] One must ask, however, how much citizen participation has been involved in the introduction of computers into our homes, our schools, and especially our jobs, up to this point. One must then ask to what extent technological decisions are likely to be subject to democratic processes, with or without a computer-literate electorate, in the future. Such decisions are now typically made in corporate or military boardrooms, far removed from public scrutiny, and there is nothing in computer literacy that will magically empower voters to alter the locus of this control. Despite talk of computers' being used to decentralize control and to offer the public unlimited access to information, there is every indication that computers are being used to further concentrate political and economic control in the hands of a few, and that the information age will mean more information for those few and far less for the rest of us. In fact, information that is now readily available to the public at no cost will soon be coming with a price tag as libraries are transformed into information brokers and videotex becomes an exclusive information resource.

Most important of all, critical debate about the social impact of computers has diminished and discussions about their toll in human values and dignity have become unfashionable, just as computer literacy has become widespread. Truly informed citizens, it seems, will not need to be computer literate in order to participate in decisions about computer technology; they will need something else.

COMPUTER LITERACY AS IDEOLOGY

It is not especially difficult to show that computer literacy is unnecessary for consumer, student, worker, or citizen in the information age. What is difficult to explain is the prevailing assumption that computer literacy *is* essential, despite the evidence to the contrary. While most people have not stopped to examine the evidence, it is nevertheless unclear how they arrived at such an assumption in the first place. What has apparently convinced an entire population that something as vague and worthless as computer literacy is essential to their lives? Why are otherwise thoughtful and intelligent teachers, journalists, labor leaders, and politicians so innocently and unthinkingly endorsing, even helping to disseminate, such pedagogical chicanery?

Cynics point with some validity to the exaggerated promotions of the computer industry as the source of this assumption. But computer merchants and manufacturers have for the most part simply exploited and enlarged on a demand that was already there. Educators, too, have been accused of exaggerating the importance of computer literacy, but they are primarily responding to pressure from parents who are concerned that their children be prepared for what they see as tomorrow's world. What amounts to a blind faith in computer literacy cannot be traced back entirely to merchants, educators, or parents, who are themselves caught up in the same assumption about the importance of computer literacy. Instead, there is something resembling ideology in all of this, an unwitting compliance, among promoters and initiates alike, with the ubiquitous imperatives of high technology: the promise of a part in a brighter economy and a grand new social order. Computer literacy seems so plausible precisely because it fits so nicely within this futuristic ideology. It might be instructive, therefore, to view the computer-literacy phenomenon not as education at all, but rather as a campaign to further envelop the population in this ideology.

The theme underlying this campaign can be extracted from the words of its most vocal advocates: Computer literacy, we are told, "leads to a favorable affective orientation"[22] that enables people to "take reasonable positions on information-related issues,"[23] "help[s] them understand the concept of compromise with respect to policy issues such as informational privacy and security,"[24] and "eliminate concerns . . . about automation in general."[25] Viewed as an ideological campaign, computer literacy seems designed to elicit public support for the present directions of computer technology. We shall see that such an interpretation contributes to a better understanding of the computer-literacy phenomenon.

Throughout the country, a small army of business leaders and educators is spreading the word about the dangers stemming from the scientific and technological illiteracy of the American people, warning that the public is not intellectually prepared to support this country in the transition to a high-technology society.[26] These leaders express their concern over opinion polls showing the public to be skeptical of technological solutions to social problems. They argue that a scientifically literate population, one knowledgeable in science and technology, would be more supportive of their high-technology prerogatives, and they call for a renewed emphasis on science and mathematics education to generate this support.

Computer-literacy education might best be construed as part of this same campaign. While its advocates tell us that their goal is to help the public become "computer comfortable," their sights seem instead to be on a population, comfortable or not, that will support the idea of an information society: "In the coming years we are going to retool our industry, and it should be made clear that we must, at the same time, retool ourselves."[27] Since, as we have seen, there is no great need for our technical retooling, this can only mean an ideological retooling, an adaptation to the imposed imperatives of high technology.

How does a computer-literacy campaign translate into support for high-technology policy? It does so in three ways. First, the form the campaign takes—its rhetoric, its intensity, its ubiquity—persuades the population that its description of the future is the correct one. Second, the content of the instruction itself—its technical emphasis, its oversimplification of issues—

eases the public into "appropriate" ways of thinking about the new technology. The third, and perhaps the most effective, means of ensuring public cooperation is the rapid institutionalization of computer literacy through the premature installation of new requirements for schooling and jobs, which literally forces the population to accept a new set of dubious realities. As we look at the form, the content, and the institutionalization of computer-literacy ideology, the heretofore disjointed landscape of the computer-literacy phenomenon begins to make sense as a coherent whole.

FORM

Ironically, the urgency surrounding computer literacy has heightened the very apprehension about computers it is supposedly designed to relieve, for although there has been a strong positive public response to computer literacy, it seems to reflect above all a fear, a panic even, of being left behind by the "computer revolution." Computer-literacy promoters have fed this anxiety with warnings that "ignorance of computers will render people as functionally illiterate as ignorance of reading, writing and arithmetic."[20] Individuals have in this way been driven to become computer comfortable by being made to feel acutely uncomfortable about their unfamiliarity with computers. This unfamiliarity, heretofore the benign consequence of intimidation, disinterest, or disdain, has become infected by the urgent necessity of computer literacy and has been transformed into a full blown fear of computers. "Computerphobia," by no coincidence, has taken on epidemic proportions just as its "antidote," computer literacy, has become available. The consequence of all this diseased emotionality is that the majority line up to take the "cure" and those left behind are seen by themselves as well as by others to be regressive relics of a suddenly distant past, their competence, their skills, their years of experience suddenly irrelevant.

Alongside this psychological layering, arguments and justifications, invalid yet persuasive, exhort consumers, students, citizens, and workers to prepare themselves for inevitable changes soon to take place in their lives. The omnipresence of the computer is used to dramatize a sense that we are in the throes of a computer revolution that will ultimately improve our society, and the routine confusion of the future with the present serves to convince the population that the information age is already upon us and therefore beyond our control. Interestingly, the very fact that there is a campaign to help people become computer literate plays a part in the dramatization of this inevitability, quite apart from any justification; for if the information age were not on the horizon, there would be no apparent reason for all this talk about computer literacy. The inevitability of a computerized society, whether it be ultimately good or bad, is by far the most important message of the computer-literacy ideology, providing, when all else fails, its argument of last resort: "It's too late to stop it."

The least defensible, yet for many the most convincing, feature of the campaign for computer literacy is its nationalistic rhetoric: "A computer-literate workforce is necessary to maintain our national defense and to improve our national productivity,"[29] we are warned, and therefore "the shortage of computer specialists and knowledge workers has raised the problem of computer literacy to the level of a national crisis."[30] Rather than examine this presumed importance of computer literacy to the nation's needs, we are encouraged instead to assume "an overarching national goal: to reverse the trend of decline of the U.S. relative to its main competition in productivity, prestige and leadership."[31]

Apparently, the current economic recession, fostering daily comparisons between ourselves and the Japanese, is the perfect mixture for such patriotic stirrings, and there is little wonder that it stifles thoughtful debate about the legitimacy of computer literacy and other high-tech solutions.

CONTENT

Focusing on the technical content of computer-literacy curricula encourages the twin mythology that high-tech jobs require high-tech skills and that high-tech politics requires high-tech expertise. The technical focus shifts attention away from social questions and portrays computers as something to learn rather than something to think about. The computer is portrayed as friendly and accessible ("Your computer likes you") and the user is encouraged to think that all computers, even those in large systems, are friendly and accessible. In this manner, computers are further mystified in the very act of demystification. Most important of all, such technical training "is a concrete basis for understanding the value of computers . . . and leads to greater acceptance of other societal applications as well."[32]

The focus on the technical also leads the user to a false sense of empowerment, "a pseudocontrol." "When you program a computer, you feel a great deal of control and mastery" because "to program a computer is to enjoy power."[33] This sense of power attracts many people to the computer, but it also deludes them into thinking that they are somehow participating in the forward momentum of computer technology when in reality they are only comforming their intellect to the configurations and constraints of computer instruction, which constitutes a new variation of "following orders." The result is a nation of citizen "computer-masters" who cannot see the forest for the trees, a perfect support system for computer technology.

The content of the social component of computer-literacy curricula serves to depoliticize debate by defining the parameters of acceptable discussion. The establishment of a carefully delineated, "safe" arena for discussions of social impact—always understood as a "break" from the real, that is, technical, focus—renders any attempt at genuine, sustained criticism illegitimate, even irrational. Above all, the public is encouraged to assume that all the important social questions have been sufficiently investigated when in fact they have been barely entertained.

INSTITUTIONALIZATION: IDEOLOGY MADE CONCRETE

As the form and the content of the campaign for computer literacy encourage support for the computer age while discouraging dissent, the population is steadily being "retooled" to fit the ideological needs of a retooled economy. Using the terminology of the technologists themselves, we might say that computer literacy is the human-factor component in the design of the information society, used to "manufacture" a computer-friendly population that is prepared to meet new user-friendly machinery halfway. Of course, most educators, businessmen, and technologists promoting computer literacy are merely unwitting participants in such ideological designs; they simply see computer literacy as a reasonable introduction to the use of an exciting new tool. There are others, however, on the national level, whose motives seem more consciously ideological.[34]

The fact that the diverse pedagogical intentions of the former fit so nicely within the ideological designs of the latter suggests that computer literacy-ideology is more hegemonic than conscious. This is confirmed by the observation that excitement over the use of the new tool is almost always accompanied by fantastical predictions of social transformation. But the best illustration of this hegemony in operation is the rapid, almost reflexive, installation of computer requirements for schooling and employment.

"The real measure of a revolution," we are assured, "is not its casualty count, but its effects on the survivors."[35] Nevertheless, computers are being used in ways that are creating a growing underclass of displaced and marginal workers. The institutionalization of computer requirements can be seen as a means—perhaps still unconscious and hegemonic—to justify those lost lives by a process of mass disqualification, which throws the blame for disenfranchisement in education and employment back on the victims themselves.

The campaign for computer literacy includes more than rhetoric and simplistic instruction; it also consists in the accelerating installation of barriers to schooling and jobs by way of credentials and hiring practices. Throughout the country, states and local districts are falling in line by establishing and standardizing high school graduation requirements in computers,[36] and colleges and universities are following the lead of Carnegie Mellon in requiring students to own their own microcomputers.[37] We are told that "teachers should be required to be computer literate before graduation [and that] knowledge of computers [should be] a criterion for employment as well."[38] Help-wanted ads for service jobs have begun to affix the recommendation "computer knowledge helpful," and magazine cover images of hard-hatted steelworkers hunched over computer keyboards serve notice that the way to a job is through computers and that he who avoids this route will have only himself to blame.

This newly manufactured need for computer literacy in order to obtain a job or get through school defies the truth that there is in fact no genuine reason to know about computers in school or in most jobs. The "need" for computer literacy has become a self-fulfilling prophecy, based not on reality but on appearance. This explains why students in poor school districts with little access to computers are in danger of becoming disenfranchised. It is not because knowledge of computers is important; rather, it is because computer credentials are now *seen* as important, and have become a needless barrier, a biased obstacle, to opportunity. Thus, a useless parcel of information about computers might determine who gets the high-tech job at the video display terminal tomorrow, just as spelling on an application determines the right candidate for a janitor's job today. Those who are already seen as marginal to the economy, often because of functional illiteracy resulting from second-rate schooling, seem destined to become doubly disqualified by being computer illiterate as well (despite the negligible difference between computer illiteracy and its opposite).

Since the new high-tech economy will involve fewer and less meaningful jobs, this installation of barriers, this reflexive concretization of ideology, will ensure that fewer applicants make the grade; computer-literacy ideology, with its own built-in justifications, will result in mass disqualification. By intensifying the already frantic competition for schooling and jobs, by reducing the numbers who will get through, and by justifying the exclusion of those who will be left behind, computer barriers impel a people to adapt themselves to the computer society, regardless of whether they are destined to become its "survivors" or its "casualties."

Knowing something about computers, tools that are apparently being used to reshape our world, would seem to be superior to remaining ignorant of them; the ideal of a technologically informed citizenry in a technological age makes sense as well. But when one considers how education for computer literacy enfeebles in the name of empowerment, mystifies in the name of demythology, and disenfranchises in the name of participation, the questions must be asked: Is it even possible in the current ideological climate to provide a potent pedagogy about computers? Is it possible to teach about computers without at the same time exaggerating their importance and without depicting their use as the highest form of intellect? Is it possible to avoid hegemonic interpretations that automatically translate the omnipresence of computers into a mythical futurism called the "information society?" Perhaps creating the space for such possibilities should become a priority among serious educators, leaving computer literacy to the ideologues. And since the computer-literacy phenomenon is but one thrust in a larger campaign to accommodate the American people to the erstwhile imperatives of high technology, our focus should perhaps be directed to this larger campaign, anticipating its further incarnations.

In recent months, for example, computer literacy has been viewed with growing disfavor, and some business leaders and educators have suggested replacing its narrow focus with a more general "basic" education, one that emphasizes critical-thinking skills, which, they say, will better prepare people to adapt to a constantly changing job market.[39] Although this appears to be a reversal of attitude toward computer literacy, it can easily be seen as a continuation of the same ideology. Since the new economy will require minimal intellectual functioning from the majority of workers, "adaptability" offers new justification for old "basic" educational policy in an economy that will no longer need many educated people. In this context, the clarion call for higher standards in the name of "excellence in education" is simply an excuse to further intensify the selection process for a streamlined economy. Most important of all, such education is still an enterprise, like computer literacy, that only further adapts a people to a world and to a future that is not of their own making.

Notes

1 Sherry Turkle, "Computer as Rorschach," *Society*, January/February 1980, p. 23.

2 Daniel Watt, "Is Computer Education Out of Control?" *Popular Computing*, August 1983, p. 84.

3 Quoted in "The Computer Moves In," *Time*, January 3, 1983, p. 24.

4 Ibid., p. 16.

5 "The Computer Moves In."

6 "Get the Jump on Tomorrow's Jobs," *Changing Times*, August 1983, p. 30.

7 "American Education: The Dead End of the Eighties," *Personal Computing*, August 1983, p. 105.

8 Ibid., p. 103.

9 See Seymour Papert, *Mindstorms: Children, Computers and Powerful Ideas* (New York: Basic Books, 1980).

10 Peter Coburn et al., *Practical Guide to Computers in Education* (Reading Mass.: Addison Wesley, 1982), p. 50.

11 Daniel H. Watt, "Education for Citizenship in a Computer-Based Society," in *Computer Literacy: Issues and Directions for 1985*, ed. Robert J. Seidel et al. (New York: Academic Press, 1982), p. 62.

12 National Commission on Excellence in Education, *A Nation at Risk: The Imperative for Educational Reform* (Washington, D.C.: U.S. Government Printing Office, April 1983), p. 26. This overnight identification of computer science as a basic skill offers a firsthand example of the ideological birth of a basic skill; it should raise our suspicions about the equally ideological origins of the more traditional basics, such as the three R's.

13 Marvin Cetron, quoted in "Get the Jump on Tomorrow's Jobs," p. 30.

14 See especially Henry M. Levin and Russell W. Rumberger, "The Educational Implications of High Technology" (Stanford Institute for Research on Educational Finance and Governance, February 1983), p. 5. See also Bob Kuttner, "The Declining Middle," *The Atlantic Monthly*, July 1983, pp. 60, 61.

15 Levin and Rumberger, "The Educational Implications of High Technology," p. 5.

16 "Schooling in 'Basics' Must Precede Computer Literacy," *Education Week*, June 15, 1983, p. 6.

17 Watt, "Is Computer Education Out of Control," p. 84.

18 See Philip Kraft, *Programmers and Managers: The Routinization of Computer Programming in the United States* (New York: Springer-Verlag, 1979).

19 "The Year of the Mouse," *Time*, January 31, 1983, p. 51.

20 Coburn et al., *Practical Guide to Computers in Education.*

21 Ronald E. Anderson, "National Computer Literacy, 1980," in Seidel, *Computer Literacy*, p. 15.

22 Andrew Molnar, "Key Components for a National Computer Literacy Program," in Seidel, *Computer Literacy*, p. 13.

23 J. C. R. Licklider, "National Goals for Computer Literacy," in Seidel, *Computer Literacy*, p. 282.

24 Ibid., p. 284.

25 Kenneth E. Brumbaugh, "Computer Literacy: 1985," in Seidel, *Computer Literacy*, p. 235.

26 See, for example, Edward B. Fiske, "New Priority: Technological Literacy," *The New York Times*, Spring Education Survey, April 23, 1983. See also the Science and Mathematics Special Supplement in *Education Week*, July 27, 1983.

27 Licklider, "National Goals," p. 282.

28 Donald Michael, quoted in Edward Fiske, "Computer Education: date '83," *Popular Computing*, August 1983, p. 94.

29 Molnar, "Key Components'" p. 3.

30 Ibid., p. 4.

31 Licklider, "National Goals."

32 Robert J. Seidel, "On the Development of an Information Handling Curriculum," in his *Computer Literacy*, p. 24.

33 Sherry Turkle, quoted in "Computers: Threat to Family?" Rochester *Times-Union*, January 8, 1983.

34 Two prominent examples: The Human Resources Research Organization (HumRRO), a major recipient of computer literacy grants and convenor of national conferences, has been funded by the Department of Education to formulate a "working definition" of computer literacy by 1984. Since HumRRO was founded by the Army in 1951 in order to "improve human performance through behavioral and social science research" (*Encyclopedia of Associations*, vol. 1 [Detroit: Gale Research, 1983], p. 421), one might ask in whose interest such a definition will be "working."

Andrew Molnar of the National Science Foundation, a leading national figure in computer literacy, wrote the U.S. Army Pamphlet 55-104 entitled *Human Factors Considerations of Undergrounds in Insurgency*, in which he asserts that "the most effective countermeasure is the use of immediate, overpowering force to repress the first signs of insurgency or resistance. Nations with a representative or constitutional form of government are often restrained from such action by moral, legal and social considerations" (p. 65). One wonders how such views are incorporated in his concern about "The Next Great Crisis in Education—Computer Literacy," the title of one of his more recent works.

35 Joseph Deken, *Electronic Cottage* (New York: Morrow, 1981), p. 2.

36 *Education Week*, February 26, 1983.

37 *Time*, January 3, 1983, p. 24.

38 David Morsund, quoted in *Education Week*, November 17, 1982, p. 16.

39 See "Schooling in 'Basics' Must Precede Computer Literacy." Also see Levin and Rumberger, "The Educational Implications of High Technology," pp. 11-13.

Computer Literacy and the Press

JOSEPH A. MENOSKY
Santa Monica, California

Recent polls indicate that some 90 percent of Americans believe that computer literacy (generally defined by proponents as a familiarity with the parts of a microcomputer and some measure of programming skill, usually in the language BASIC) is important enough to warrant its inclusion in the national educational curriculum. Other articles in this issue examine the validity of this belief, and suggest that the promises of the computer literati—for more and better jobs, for a profoundly deeper educational experience, and for citizen empowerment—have no basis in reality. This article is concerned with how and why the belief itself has been propagated by the American news media.

Certainly those who have a great deal to gain from a universal acceptance of computer literacy—microcomputer firms selling hardware, textbook companies selling educational software, organizations selling worker and teacher retraining courses, and writers and publishers selling books and instructional guides—have done a brilliant, if morally indefensible, job of commercial promotion. But their unsupported claims have been buttressed at all times by an almost completely uncritical press coverage that provided, in essence, free advertising in the guise of objective reporting. The press therefore must bear a substantial measure of the blame for the recent hysteria.

This is not surprising given the traditionally poor response of the popular science media to complex technological issues, but rarely has the press offered its unqualified blessing to a dubious project that has such vast implications for public policy. This analysis of press support for the computer-literacy movement will focus on how information about science and technology in general flows through the popular media, and how certain aspects of reporting color that information. Coverage of computer literacy will be discussed in that light, and reference will be made to specific examples.

Over the past two decades, popular interest in science and technology has grown, as has a subset of the general news media known as "science journalism." Though coverage appears widespread—science and technology features can be found in countless newspapers and magazines and on television and radio—in fact, the overwhelming majority of stories are derived from the same few sources. Primary sources of information—academic journals, scientific meetings, and the like—are covered by such large newspapers as the *New York Times*, the *Washington Post*, and the *Wall Street*

Journal, and by wire services such as United Press International and Associated Press. This coverage usually becomes source material for monthly magazines and radio and television networks, which in turn are themselves sources for local papers, television, and radio.

At every level of this chain, reporters, if not copying each other directly, are following the same leads, calling the same "experts," and asking the same questions. Not long ago a science story well over a year out of date spread like wildfire across the country due to a mistakenly issued press release from the National Science Foundation that nobody bothered to confirm. If it is in the *Times,* it is news. And it is news everywhere. Of the relatively small number of science reporters who do originate most of the stories, few see themselves as critics of the uses and abuses of science and technology. Rather, they see themselves in the role of educator, explaining and describing an aspect of modern life to an interested audience. (One large-circulation popular science magazine actually has an editorial injunction against saying anything "bad" about technology.)

This structural tendency toward a boosterism that echoes throughout the popular media is pushed even further by computer technology. The primary sources that many reporters draw on for information about this field—*Byte* magazine, *Popular Computing, Personal Computing,* and so forth—are themselves secondary sources that exist expressly to promote the use of computers. A popular treatment of some aspect of computer technology that relies on such publications will almost inevitably be skewed in the same direction. Given the incestuous way in which information moves through the system, this promotional bias will be propagated nationwide.

The extent to which this institutional phemomenon was responsible for fueling the computer-literacy mania should not be underestimated, but it still does not explain how, at the individual level, reporters are able to consistently get away with bad journalism. This can be answered by examining the media response to an single event: Harvard University's conference "Video Games and Human Development," held at that institution in the spring of 1983. The conference and the way it was reported constitute an almost perfect miniature of the media's general obsession with computer literacy. After three days of speakers, the message was clear for all the nations to hear: Computer games represent the single most profound educational breakthrough in the history of the species.

This bold claim was almost universally and unreservedly reiterated by the major magazines, newspapers, and television and radio stations that sent representatives to the conference (possibly the only two exceptions were a highly critical report in *Newsweek* and a satirical attack by the author in *Science 83*).[1]

The extensive positive coverage serves to illustrate one of the prevailing principles of the popular media: A new angle sells. The video-game phenomenon had been all over the newsstands and the airwaves a year before the conference, but there are only so many ways to write about Pac-Man, and an audience will only sit still for a relatively limited number of excursions by Action News camera teams into the local arcade. Once the novelty angle was exhausted, the video game was no longer news.

As the site of the first academic conference on the subject, Harvard provided a new angle—the educational potential of video games. Since a report saying that video games have little or no educational merit would have been something of a nonstory at that time (a bit like saying "the White House was not painted blue today"), the easiest way to "make news" was to say that they do. (The other alternative was to cover the conference as a newsworthy event in itself—the approach taken by the critical pieces in *Newsweek* and *Science 83*.)

This is very much the pattern taken in the coverage of computer literacy. By the close of 1982, personal computers had been all the rage in the media (*Time* magazine's "Machine of the Year," etc.), but the subject was getting stale. The educational uses of computers and the need for computer literacy quickly became the angle that generated at least another year's worth of additional news features about microcomputer technology.

All of this blatant boosterism might appear at odds with the myth of the objective reporter who painstakingly tries to uncover "all sides" of a story, and it is. But science reporters in particular have a mechanism for dealing with that contradiction. Rae Goodell, who teaches science writing at M.I.T., has termed this the "artificial dichotomy."[2] A bold claim for the benefits of a given technology is held up against an extreme cautionary statement about its potential risks. Since the latter is almost always chosen and phrased by the reporter to look ridiculous, it is easily discarded. Any murky or disturbing details are conveniently ignored, and the discussion proper swings over to extolling the alleged benefits. The artificial dichotomy serves the ideal of "balanced" reporting because it seemingly presents "both sides," but it still allows for the unbridled trumpeting of unsupported—even insupportable—claims of benefits.

In the *Washington Post* and the *Boston Globe*, and in a *Time* magazine article from the Harvard conference that epitomizes almost everything bad about popular science reporting, the artificial dichotomy is established in the very first paragraph.

> Video games, reviled as a scourge of American youth, may be taking a bad rap.[3]

> Video games are not ruining American families. Coast-to-coast arcades are neither a menace to the kids who cram them nor to society at large.[4]

> Ever since the first pong was pinged, video games have been accused of increasing crime and school absenteeism, decreasing learning and concentration, and causing a mysterious ailment called video wrist. But

according to a conference sponsored last week by the Harvard Graduate School of Education, the mothers and fathers of River City may breathe easier. Researchers and scientists suggested that video games may turn out to be one of the most powerful teaching tools ever devised.[5]

All three of these examples set up false oppositions. "Video wrist" and the ruination of the American family are in no way related to the potential of the video game as a teaching instrument. Disproving or making sport of the former claim does nothing to increase the legitimacy of the latter. The artificial dichotomy creates the illusion that it does. It also successfully defuses all possible critics by pigeonholing them, in this case, as "the mothers and fathers of River City"—an irrational and silly bunch of reactionaries. The choice of emotionally loaded words: "*menace* . . . to society," "*reviled* as a *scourge* of American youth," reinforces this image. The reader is asked, in essence, to identify with the small-minded rubes or with the proponents of progress. Given that formulation, it is not difficult to predict how the majority will choose.

Coverage of the computer-literacy movement in general has been characterized by a less blatant but more insidious variety of this approach that allows for a debate, but effectively keeps it within narrowly established limits. The lead to another *Washington Post* article from the Harvard conference well illustrates this particular sleight of hand: "Computerizing the nation's classrooms—far from being all fun and games—poses difficult questions of social equity and massive teacher training, educators were warned today."[6]

The truly difficult questions about whether or not the nation's classrooms *should* be computerized are neatly finessed. Instead, discussion is limited to *how* this process should take place. The very existence of critics who dispute the value of computer education is denied.

Again, the choice of words prompts the reader to identify with the writer's own biases. "Social equity" is a good liberal term that nevertheless posits a narrow range of public policy choices: Either we allow computer literacy to flourish only in the wealthier, white schools, thus putting poorer, minority groups at a further disadvantage, or we support computer-literacy programs for everybody. Who but a bigot would choose the former over the latter?

Avoided, of course, is even a cursory examination of whether computer literacy represents a basic skill so profoundly important as to justify the multibillion dollar public programs required to promote it. The real social equity tragedy is that one more racial and class barrier is being erected without any justification and in the complete absence of public debate. The child from a high school that could not afford to offer six months of programming in BASIC may be barred from college or from a job, even if programming in BASIC is irrelevant to future performance. By limiting the range of discussion, the media have excluded this fundamentally important issue, and set an agenda for all future debate.

The almost pathological inability of the popular science media to take a historical perspective—even in the most limited sense—makes a full airing of the issues even less likely. Certain crucial aspects of a technological issue simply cannot be appreciated by a reporter on deadline who is concerned solely with what happens in the ever-present now. Coverage of the Harvard video-game conference is a case in point. According to *Time*:

> Underwritten in part with a $40,000 grant from Atari, "Video games and Human Development: A Research Agenda for the '80s" represented one of the first attempts to organize the nascent and often flimsy research done on the subject so far.[7]

Though at the time it was not yet common knowledge, anyone even remotely familiar with the video-game industry realized that the craze had hit its peak over half a year before the conference. Arcades were closing, and both coin-operated and home-game manufacturers were taking a severe beating in the marketplace. For all its academic trappings, the Harvard conference represented an attempt by the beleaguered Atari to open up new markets for its products. By emphasizing the educational and even psychological and social-curative powers of computer games, the company hoped to create a need for them in the schools, mental hospitals, and neighborhood halfway houses. The firm actually supplied Harvard with the names of potential speakers, some of whom had conducted studies supported by Atari funds. Harvard, in turn, was desperately trying to get its own computers and education program off the ground, and saw the conference as a way to generate interest. This hidden "research agenda," again, was painfully obvious to anyone slightly knowledgeable about video games, or at all aware of the recent tendency toward increasingly closer "partnerships" between industry and academe.

Almost every news feature concerned with the educational aspects of computers has suffered from this ahistorical bias toward the new. The use of computers in education has a long and checkered past that is rarely if ever acknowledged. Despite the flashy visuals and sounds that accompany the latest generation of educational software, almost all computer-aided instruction is based on a "programmed-instruction" workbook method that predates Sputnik. For over two decades computer variations on this basic theme have been hailed time and again as the greatest breakthrough in educational technology, and the culture has yet to see any evidence for that claim. In the absence of a historical perspective, the media will be content to repeat that hyperbole indefinitely.

Many of the established science writers at least have some command of a technical field, even if they are unabashedly given to its promotion. The same cannot be said for most of those who write about computer technology. Because the computer has such a wide variety of applications, it is covered by everyone from business reporters to entertainment critics to human-interest columnists. In principle there is nothing wrong with this, but in fact, what often happens is that a reporter with depth in a nontechnological area ends up perpetuating misconceptions or unsupported claims because he or she either does not know any better or is not accustomed to asking certain questions.

At the Harvard conference reporters actually managed to fabricate entirely new misconceptions. Sylvia Weir, a presenter from M.I.T., described her work with severely disabled individuals and the computer language LOGO. Weir, who privately expressed puzzlement at her invitation to the conference, publicly emphasized that LOGO should not be confused with video games.

Time magazine promptly wrote: "Sylvia Weir, a research associate at M.I.T., showed a film of an educational video game in which the user experiences the principles of Newtonian physics."[8]

According to the *Washington Post*:

> Sylvia Weir, a pediatrician who runs a computer project at the Massachusetts Institute of Technology, reported on advances made with cerebral palsy victims, who have used computer games to overcome communications obstacles. One 7-year-old boy who was incapable of speaking used a keyboard "to tell us what he was doing in terms of what the [game] was doing." Weir has also used games to help dyslexic children overcome their reading disorders.[9]

Given this sort of performance by the Fourth Estate, the general public's confusion vis-à-vis the claims made for computer technology is not at all surprising.

Some of this nonsense, which wastes vast public resources and obscures the real causes of poor education and unemployment, could be avoided if the press took a more rigorous attitude toward science and technology. Political issues are heatedly debated daily in the popular news media; the deeply political and social aspects of science and technology should be approached in the same way. There is nothing wrong with telling people how things work, but this should not be the extent of science journalism. A more critical perspective is also appropriate.

It is not even necessary to have a deep expertise in a field so long as both reporters and audience realize that there are some basic questions that can be asked about any technology and its social impact. The implementation of a technology, for instance, has certain costs and benefits. What are they and, more importantly, how are they distributed? Rarely if ever do those who have the most to gain also have the most to lose. Those who do have the most to gain may well be the loudest proponents of a technology. If so, they should be identified as such. Is there any evidence to back up the claims of benefits? Proponents should bear the burden of proof, especially if substantial public sums are involved. An estimation of costs should include, in addition to any immediate financial outlay, maintenance and other support, and a discussion of potential social costs. Are there other, possibly more effective ways of dealing with the problem (including other technologies) that will be ignored if the proposed technology is implemented?

Unfortunately, it is a little too late to apply these principles to the computer-literacy movement. Its gospel has become a powerful social force that probably could not be dispelled at this time even with an all-out attack by the news media—as unlikely as that would be. Advertisers have done their job too well, and the press has too freely given its blessing. All that is left is for the craze to be played out, and in a year or two when it becomes clear that an Apple in every classroom represents something a good deal less than an educational or economic revolution, interest will wane. In the absence of a critical approach, some other new miracle machine will be enshrined. At this time, interactive videodisc technology appears to be the strongest contender, but look for a surprise entry from the Japanese.

Notes

1 "Video Games Zap Harvard," *Newsweek*, June 6, 1983, p. 92; and Joseph Menosky, "The Emperor's New Video Game," *Science 83*, October 1983, p. 83.

2 Rae Goodell, "The Gene Craze," *Columbia Journalism Review*, November/December 1980.

3 Vivian Aplin-Brownlee, "Zap! Gulp! Video Game Critics Hit from Top Sides," *Washington Post*, June 1983, p. A3.

4 Judy Forman, "Early Findings: Video Games Getting Bad Rap," *Boston Globe*, May 24, 1983, p. 17.

5 "Donkey Kong Goes to Harvard," *Time*, June 6, 1983, p. 77.

6 Vivian Aplin-Brownlee, "Ways Sought to Turn Arcade Fascination into Better Education," *Washington Post*, May 25, 1983, p. A2.

7 *Time*, June 6, 1983.

8 Ibid.

9 Tom Zito, "Arguing for the Arcade," *Washington Post*, May 24, 1983, p. B1.

Heading for the Ha-Ha

BRIAN SIMPSON
London, England

THE HA-HA

A ha-ha is a sunken fence, invisible from a distance, allowing a tantalizing, unobstructed view of the verdant pastures on the other side, but forming an impenetrable barrier. There is a ha-ha surrounding educational technology. My aim in this article is to investigate its nature and to see if anything can, or should, be done about it.

Technological solutions to educational problems often have a seductive appeal, promising to make education easier and more enjoyable than ever before. In the past, extravagant claims have been made for teaching machines, educational television, language laboratories, and even such improbable, esoteric phenomena as sleep learning and learning under music-induced hypnosis. Most of these failed, however, to fulfill their early promise. And some went the way of the dodo.

Predicting the future of educational technology is not easy: The most consistent finding in such forecasting, as in economic forecasting, is that things do not turn out as predicted. To improve the accuracy of our forecasts for the future of the new technology, we should first try to understand why we have come to use the existing technology the way we do. (Here I use the word *technology* in its widest sense, to include traditional classroom teaching.) The commonest methodological failing of technological futurologists is to consider the future without due reference to the past.

PEOPLE ARE NOT MACHINES

We do not have to look far to discover the reasons for what many regard as the disappointing rate of progress in educational technology. Education is the development of people, and people are not machines, or even machinelike. Our need to make sense of an increasingly confusing world of men and machines often leads us to blur the distinction, first in the way we speak and then in the way we act. We anthropomorphize machines ("electronic brain") and we "mechanomorphize" people ("What makes them tick?"), and we

This article is adapted from an article which first appeared in the British Journal of Educational Technology, *vol. 14, no. 1, 1983, published by the Council for Educational Technology, London.*

allow ergonomics, the philanthropic science of adapting machines to people, to merge into a darker science of adapting people to machines.

Since educational technology operates at the person-machine interface, it is salutary to consider what makes people so essentially nonmachinelike. People are not simply clusters of atoms and subatomic particles that bounce off one another in accordance with the laws of physics. We have conscious experience. Indeed, there is a school of thought—subjective idealism—in which nothing exists *except* conscious experience. "It is indeed an opinion *strangely* prevailing amongst men, that houses, mountains, rivers, and in a word all sensible objects have an existence natural or real, distinct from their being perceived by the understanding."[1] Machines, by contrast, are not conscious: They can receive input but they cannot perceive it; they can be damaged but they cannot be in pain. Also, because we believe (for no logically defensible reason) that other people resemble us internally, we can empathize, that is, we have an intuitive understanding of the conscious experience of others. Another significant fact is revealed by the parenthesized phrase above: We do not need to be logical. We have other modes of intelligent thought.

These and other important differences between people and machines make person-machine interactions quite unlike person-person ones. A machine only ever responds; it does not initiate. Furthermore, its responses are either totally rigid or random in an unmistakably machinelike way. Machines have no subtlety. Moreover, a machine is incapable of satisfying social needs; people need people in ways in which they do not need machines. Machines cannot be warm, sympathetic, or encouraging. They can be made to pretend to be, but it is just a pretense: Machines have nothing like a right-hand cerebral hemisphere. This all leads to problems when educators try to substitute machines for teachers. It makes sense to use machines only to *support* teachers, not to replace or mimic them.

COMPUTERS IN EDUCATION

Computers are no different in principle from other machines, despite their remarkable capacity for storing, retrieving, and manipulating data. The quaint anthropomorphic catch-phrase "electronic brain" was popular in the early days of computers; now, to a more sophisticated public, it sounds either hyperbolic or plainly absurd. Computers are not brains, nor do they have brains. They do not think; they process. They are lighting-fast and totally infallible, but they are mindless.

It is for these reasons that computer-assisted instruction (CAI) has rumbled along the runway for years now, not quite able to take off. CAI has been frequently misunderstood. It cannot be sensibly used as a substitute for either teachers or books, although it has often been used for both.

Of course, computers can be programmed to do *some* of the things that teachers do—for example, give information, exercises, and tests—but they cannot deal with unexpected questions or unprogrammed misunderstandings. Human educators—instructors, trainers, tutors—are intuitively able to do this rather well, but intuition cannot, by definition, be programmed. Also, although a computer screen can be used for displaying text, it is an uncomfortable and unsatisfactory substitute for the pages of a book.

In general, the essential limitations of computers are revealed not by what computers do, but by what they fail to do. "Artificial intelligence" is often a deceit: nothing more than the artificial mimicry of people behaving in limited modes. A good example is the famous "Doctor" program, described by Weizenbaum, which enables a patient to converse, via a keyboard, with a computerized "psychiatrist."[2] The fact that this should be possible, or at least seem possible, is evidence for the simplistic nature of nondirective psychotherapy, not for the intelligence of computers.

Even if a CAI student were fooled into thinking that a tutor rather than a computer was responding to his terminal input, it would not be like his having a *conversation* with a tutor. Computers are limited in the ways in which they can deal with data: Their stock in trade is not education, but facts. Of course, some learning of facts is necessary, but it is hardly the essence of education; it is a peripheral need. CAI programs tend to encourage the convergent, atomistic view of education that is characteristic of some conventional teaching. Hudson criticizes this approach thus: "As a student, I was certainly left with the belief that all knowledge consisted of *facts*: hard little nuggets of reality that one could assemble like building blocks into patterns. . . . Whatever its virtues, the atomistic habit of mind is ill-adapted to the elusive, shifting world of everyday meanings."[3]

Even more important than the learning that accompanies CAI is metalearning. CAI is the product of an educational ideology that insists that there are right and wrong answers, and that a wrong answer contains nothing of interest. The reality is not so simple. Most "facts" are nothing more than points of view, and most "wrong" answers are full of useful information about how a person sees the world (not just about what is wrong with the way he sees it).

The right/wrong ideology is by no means the exclusive preserve of computers: It has been maintained in the past by generations of bad teachers and by the authors of those ghastly programmed instructional (PI) texts that languish in educational storerooms, gathering dust. It is, however, an ideology that computers are particularly well suited to propagate. CAI cannot help with the more serious and more romantic ideals of education set out by Whitehead: "Culture is activity of thought, and receptiveness of beauty and humane feeling. Scraps of information have nothing to do with it. A merely well-informed man is the most useless bore on God's earth."[4]

Another important ideological perspective was discussed by Freire: "If our option is *for man*, education is cultural actions for freedom and therefore an act of knowing and not of memorization."[5] Computers *can* help students in the pursuit of such genuine knowledge, as explained in the next section, but it is often easier to use computers (in CAI mode) to assist simple acts of memorization. There is a consequent tendency for the latter to become the dominant application.

WHAT ARE COMPUTERS GOOD FOR?

Despite these caveats about CAI, there is good news as well as bad about the use of computers in education. Computers are versatile educational *aids*. They can be used to simulate a great variety of processes—economic, mechanical, physical, chemical, and so forth—and they can also be used to perform complex and otherwise time-consuming calculations. Furthermore, they are useful for recording students' progress, for administering and scoring objective tests, and for directing students to appropriate parts of a curriculum. (This is what is known as computer-managed learning or CML.)

When used as simulators or calculators, computers can provide valuable processing power and can even help students to develop new insights. They enable students to test hypotheses, to investigate the effect of varying parameters on dependent variables, and to explore and compare a variety of possible experimental outcomes without, before, or as well as actually doing the experiments. When a student is driving a computer it is a tool for creativity and discovery. Only when computers drive students, as they do in CAI, do they risk becomings tools for the mindless rote of acquisition of "knowledge."

The late Nevill Coghill, Oxford Professor of English, was quite right when he said, "It's clear that computers can never be tutors."[6] If we fall into the trap of using computers as substitute tutors they will simply end up like the teaching machines of the past—hidden away, unloved and forgotten. It would be a shame to destroy the educational reputation of computers simply by casting them in the wrong role.

EDUCATIONAL TELEVISION

Television has been used in various ways in education, ranging from closed-circuit transmissions within a building to long-distance broadcasts via satellites. It enables a remote audience of unlimited size to see something happening in a studio, in a lecture theater, or in the "real world." The audience can be remote both in time and place. All too often the audience is also remote in spirit.

An attempt in the late 1960s to use television in IBM (UK) Education demonstrated some of its most serious shortcomings. At that time it was used to relay live lectures from a studio to several adjacent classrooms. The purpose here was to enable audiences too large to be accommodated in one classroom to "attend" the lectures, and it was hoped that this would improve the lecturers' productivity. Some student-lecturer communication was made possible by providing students with a signaling button and a voice link. One-way lecturing of this kind was, however, found to be extremely disconcerting, both for lecturers and students, and by no means easy to handle.

An effective lecturer is aware of and responsive to the reactions of his students; this is not possible for someone lecturing in the vacuum of a studio. Also, an important motivator for students is the atmosphere created in the room by the lecturer. The same kind of atmosphere is not created by a televised talking head. Lecturers found teaching into a camera very wearing. The result of the IBM experiments was that students were bored; they lost concentration and ended up doing crossword puzzles or finding other ways of amusing themselves. Lecturers would occasionally visit classrooms toward the end of an afternoon to find that half of their students had gone. Productivity measured in student days per lecturer day might have been boosted, but measured in terms of student achievement the experiments were a failure. They were eventually discontinued.

It is significant that the Open University, which has access to the considerable resources of BBC, has found that educational television broadcasts are a minor educational vehicle, the cost of which often far exceeds the benefit. The main educational medium of the Open University is the study text.

The only situation in which television has an important edge over alternative media is where a remote student audience is shown something it could not otherwise see (say the behavior of wildlife in a distant country, the inside of a nuclear reactor, or a lecture by a uniquely brilliant lecturer), or where it is used to record an activity for immediate replay and analysis—as it is for the training of teachers.[7]

RECORDED VIDEO

The recent invention of videodisc has sparked renewed interest in the potential of recorded video as an educational medium, particularly when players are linked to interactive computer systems. The intrinsic interest of the medium must not, however, distract us from the important task of understanding precisely how, if at all, it should be employed for educational purposes.

Videodiscs look like gramophone records. They are played on a machine that feeds into a conventional television set rather the same way as videocassettes. Some have two sound tracks—used for alternative languages or stereo. Like gramophone records, they are "read-only," but unlike gramophone records they can be made to go in slow motion, they can "freeze" to display a still picture, and they can even be played backward. The storage capacity of the discs is remarkable. Typically, a single videodisc will either play for half an hour per side in "continuous" mode or will display over

50,000 still frames—full screen pictures—per side. Each frame is addressable by keying in its frame number using a keypad (which looks like a pocket calculator). Some players contain simple microprocessors, and some can be interfaced with independent computers, allowing sophisticated interactive programming.

Video recording and replay technology (videocassette and videodisc), in common with educational television, is most useful for applications where it is important for the student to see what things look like. Suitable applications include the training of doctors in symptomatology and surgery, the training of car mechanics in vehicle dismantling and reassembly, and the training of electronic technicians in tracing and rectifying faults. Much education is about ideas rather than appearance, however, and ideas are learned primarily through words and symbols, not pictures. Diagrams, graphs, and visual metaphors of various kinds can be used to enhance such education, but they only support the printed or spoken word; they cannot replace it.

High quality visual teaching aids might eventually be made available on videodisc, perhaps with animation, and projected in the classroom using large screen television projectors. Such discs could also contain spoken commentaries. They would assist the teacher in much the same way that educational films currently help him. The special playback facilities—addressable frame access, slow motion, freeze-frame, and reverse—would have a few, but only a few, obvious applications, particularly in the teaching of sports such as swimming and tennis.

A more powerful way of using videodisc is to allow each student to interact with his own videodisc player, either using its built-in microprocessor or under the control of an independent computer. This is an expensive approach to education, both in hardware and software. Although it might have a future in some areas of industrial, commercial, and professional training, it is unlikely to find its way into our schools or universities—at least not unless there were a boom in the medium, which would almost certainly have to originate in the entertainment market. This could lead to the same kind of dramatic fall in hardware costs that has enabled television to become such a widely used educational aid. IBM is, however, already using interactive computer-linked videodiscs for training computer engineers, and Hon gives a superb example of their use for teaching people how to perform cardiopulmonary resuscitation.[8]

BETTER CLASSROOMS

> A discussion of teaching aids may seem like an unusual context in which to consider a teacher's role in teaching. Yet, withal, the teacher constitutes the principal aid in the teaching process.[9]

Since, as is indisputably the case, human teachers will be the main educational technology of the future, as they have been in the past, we need to develop more efficient models of classroom education. The ancient ritual of teachers' standing in front of classes "teaching," and hoping that this will somehow result in learning, has gone on for long enough. So has the teaching of academic and abstract subjects (such as calculus, Shakespeare, and French grammar) to young children who have no earthly use for them, except to jump over meaningless examination hurdles in an incomprehensible scramble for "qualifications."

Enough is known from studies of human learning, motivation, and other related areas of psychological research for us to realize the importance of teaching the right things, at the right level, at the right time. And "right" here means congruent with the child's perception of his or her own needs and interests. Teacher does not know best.

Too many of today's classrooms—in industry and commerce as well as in schools—bear an uncomfortably close resemblance to Victorian classrooms. Students are too passive and teachers talk too much. Effective education needs to be centered on appropriate learning activities. We need to develop new rituals in which the teachers do less teaching and do more organizing and controlling of student-centered learning.

This has, of course, been said before (most eloquently by Postman and Weingartner[10]), but little has been done about it. It would need significant investment in teacher training to bring about significant changes and spending money on this kind of human development may be difficult when the current wisdom dictates that it should be spent on chips. Unless we spend the money on people, however, money spent on chips is money down the drain.

Recognition of the importance of better classroom teaching must go hand-in-hand with an appreciation of the high relative cost of teachers. They should not waste their valuable time doing the things technology can do better and more cheaply. It would be easy to swing from seeing technology as a panacea to seeing it as anathema: easy, but absurd.

THE EDUCATIONAL SUPER-MEDIUM

What educational device can be used by a man on the Clapham omnibus without disturbing the other passengers? (Clue: It has no batteries, it is cheap and silent, and it contains data that can be sequentially or directly accessed.) The answer: a book. No technology has come anywhere near matching it for versatility, economy, and effectiveness. It has been increasingly widely used for education since Gutenberg invented his printing press in 1457. It has survived the introduction of radio and television; it will equally survive the onslaught of the silicon chip.

Microchip technology will, of course, help us to produce better books, and this may well turn out to be its most useful educational role. The direct use of word processors by authors facilitates effective and creative writing and obviates transcription errors. Computerized proofreading also helps to eliminate spelling mistakes and it can be used to draw attention to the use of jargon, or clumsy or ungrammatical constructions. Of course, it is not foolproof, and it does not compensate for the deficiencies of someone who cannot write. The original of this article was electronically proofread, so the evidence is before you! Nor does it obviate critical thought. My electronic proofreader suggested that Nevill Coghill was misspelled, and offered Negligee Cowgirl as an alternative. It also thought filmstrips was a misprint for flimsies. Computers may be mindless, but they can apparently still have fetishes! Accepting these limitations—and there was never a pro without a con—electronic word processing certainly makes it easier for an author to pay attention to what he wants to say, leaving the business of grammatical, syntactical, and structural massaging until later. Far from heralding the end of the era of printed text, the invention of the silicon chip might well be heralding a new beginning.

Regardless of the excitement generated by new developments in educational technology, many of the most important questions about education remain unanswered. As Lawless of the Open University puts it, we have "new chips but old problems": Microelectronic technology will not make teaching, or preparing instruction, any easier; "quite the reverse will be the case . . . equipment will be unused, underused, or be used to convey existing models of teaching, unsuited to the new devices."[11] It is clear that the development of technology is easily outpacing the development of educational know-how.

There will be no sudden boom in new forms of educational technology: In that respect the future is set to resemble the past.

> Estimating how educational technology may develop over the next 20 years is perhaps best begun by reflecting on what has happened over the past two decades . . . the great expectations of the 1950s have not been fulfilled. . . . Hardware development has proceeded much faster than software development. Quality instructional materials for use with available hardware are lacking. . . . Hardware alone is not enough.[12]

But if hardware alone is not enough, neither is the combination of hardware and software. Education still needs teachers and it also needs books. Modern technology neither destroys nor transforms the traditional context of education; it simply augments it.

Provided that we understand the limitations of each technology as well as its capabilities, and, more importantly, provided that we understand the people we are trying to educate and the kind of education we are trying to give them, we can use technology in ways that will really help. There is no technological panacea; there are only technological solutions to *some* educational problems. But if we start imagining that technology can bring about a quick and easy methodological revolution we shall be heading straight for the ha-ha.

Notes

1 Bishop G. Berkeley, *A Treatise Concerning the Principles of Human Knowledge,* 1710.

2 J. Weizenbaum, *Computer Power and Human Reason* (San Francisco: W. H. Freeman, 1976).

3 L. Hudson, *The Cult of the Fact* (London: Jonathan Cape, 1970).

4 A. N. Whitehead, *The Aims of Education* (London: Ernest Benn, 1950).

5 P. Freire, *Cultural Action for Freedom* (Harmondsworth, Eng.: Penguin Books, 1972).

6 This is from an unpublished poem (1965) addressed to Ken Segar, Fellow of St. Edmund Hall, Oxford. The full text was "It's clear that computers/Can Never be Tutors;/What *we* want is *men*/Especially Ken!"

7 D. W. Allen and K. A. Ryan, *Microteaching* (Reading, Mass.: Addison-Wesley, 1969).

8 D. Hon, "Interactive Training in Cardiopulmonary Resuscitation," *Byte* 7, no. 6 (1982): 108–38.

9 J. Bruner, *The Process of Education* (Cambridge: Harvard University Press, 1960).

10 N. Postman and C. Weingartner, *Teaching as a Subversive Activity* (Harmondsworth, Eng.: Penguin Books, 1971).

11 C. Lawless, "New Chips but Old Problems," in *Education Technology to the Year 2000,* ed. R. Winterburn and L. Evans (London: Kogan Page, 1980).

12 R. E. Burns and W. I. Davisson, "The Use of Filmstrips and Records and Computer-Aided Instruction," in *Education Technology to the Year 2000,* ed. Winterburn and Evans.

The Technological Threat to Education

ROBERT J. SARDELLO
Dallas Institute of Humanities and Culture

I am going to talk about computers and the promised revolution in education attendant on the arrival of a promised computer culture. I want to expose the utopian fantasies inherent in all talk of computers' revolutionizing education, and right at the start, so you will know where I stand, I am firmly opposed to the introduction of the computer as a technological device oriented toward changing the very tradition of education. Now, this may seem to be a very close-minded position, not at all like a practicing psychologist who almost always has trouble saying whether anything is right or wrong. But this evaluation is not a prejudice, a prejudgment. It comes out of a great deal of consideration of what kind of thing the computer is, and a great deal of consideration of the relation between technology and culture. And the conclusion that I have come to may surprise you. The computer, if it is allowed to infiltrate the very heart of education in the particular manner I will outline in a moment, will destroy education: not because it is a mechanism, and as such threatens to transform human beings into likenesses of itself; the destructive power of the computer is to be found in the fact that it transforms education into psychology. Furthermore, the peculiar kind of psychology that characterizes the computer is a psychological symptom, and the symptom is that of the psychopath. In other words, if the kind of computer education that I am about to outline actually comes about, we will be transformed into a culture of psychopaths.

So, having started with a conclusion, a conclusion that I trust has evoked your attention, let me try to demonstrate that I know whereof I speak. First, let us establish the particular kind of computer education that is a threat to the whole of Western culture. Computers used as technical devices to perform operations that are themselves technical are not included as threatening to culture. Pocket calculators, word processors, and all the variety of programs that are ready-made for use in personal computers do not pose a threat to the very meaning of education. These technical devices can free the imagination for the consideration of matters involving mathematics, accounting, economics, or business. Or, in the case of word processing, the imagination is set free to focus on the craft of writing itself.

What is called "computer-assisted instruction" also does not pose a real threat to culture. Teaching machines or programmed instruction have already shown themselves to be dismal failures, precisely because they turn the learner into a mechanism, who duly responds with frustration and boredom.

The technological threat to education is to be found in the claim that teaching the child to program the computer can be done in such a manner that programming teaches the processes of thinking itself and thus removes the necessity of formal classroom instruction. Such a claim has been put forth by Seymour Papert, the Cecile Greene Professor of Education at M.I.T., inventor of the system of programming called LOGO, which is rapidly finding its way into educational settings. These are the claims set forth by Papert:

> I see the classroom as an artificial and inefficient learning environment that society has been forced to invent because its informal environments fail in certain essential domains, such as writing or grammar or school math. I believe that the computer presence will enable us to so modify the learning environment outside the classroom that much if not all the knowledge schools presently try to teach with such pain and expense and such limited success will be learned, as the child learns to talk, painlessly, successfully, and without organized instruction. This obviously implies that schools as we know them today will have no place in the future.[1]

> Of course, LOGO can help in the teaching of traditional curriculum, but I have thought of it as a vehicle for Piagetian learning [that is, following the system of the Swiss psychologist, Jean Piaget], which to me is learning without curriculum.

> I see Piaget as the theorist of learning without curriculum and the theorist of the kind of learning that happens without deliberate teaching. To turn him into the theorist of a new curriculum is to stand him on his head.[2]

> But "teaching without curriculum" does not mean spontaneous, free-form classroom or simply "leaving the child alone." It means supporting children as they build their own intellectual structures with materials drawn from the surrounding culture.[3]

These claims are radical. We need to be prepared to accept them if they can indeed produce a genuine reform in public education. The radicality of the claims makes them most appealing. There is no patchwork on a system of education dictated by the system itself here, with all the built-in protections to assure that the system remains relatively intact. These claims offer a true revolution in education. Is it, however, a revolution that renews the roots of culture and tradition or one that will destroy the memory of culture altogether?

Teaching children to program computers in school does not have as its aim the introduction of a new subject matter into education. Computer programming, as outlined in the LOGO system, is not subject-centered but child-centered. It is the ultimate extension of the methods course now so prevalent in teacher education, for, in a significant way, it eliminates content altogether and reduces all education to method; all things can be learned through the method of computer programming. So, it is necessary to be aware of the false claim that argues that computers must be introduced into schools because we are entering a time when anyone who does not know programming will be illiterate in a computer culture. The very term *computer literacy* establishes the computer as far more than a machine; such a term is an assault on the basis of culture itself by assuming that computer programming is truly a language—not a constructed, artificial language, but a language fully capable of expressing the full and complete life of a people. There is a huge inflation to the suggestion that the artificial terminology of computer programming constitutes a language at all. It assumes that language no longer emanates from the life of a community, from geographical place, from heritage, ritual, from the living body of a people, from the voice of things in the world. The new origins of culture, so the inflated claim would state, are IBM, Apple, Xerox, and Texas Instruments. Computer terminology is certainly not a living language, but rather the enslaving of language by turning every form of speech into an object to be manipulated by the totalitarian grammar of computational logic.

The computer looms before us as far more than a device for presenting, in "programmed style," traditional subject matter to be learned. The claim that we are entering into a computer culture must be clearly understood and taken quite seriously, in spite of all of its falseness. Culture is never a progressive affair. Culture always comes about by looking backward, by recovering the past, by relating the present to permanent patterns of the soul, by remembering the dead, by reflection of values. The aim of introducing programming into the schools is to forget the past, not to renew it.

We must realize, however, that the claims of programming carry any persuasive power at all because true, living culture is itself nearly dead. Education has not done its job, the primary job of schooling, which is the initiation of the young into the life of culture. As Donald Cowan pointed out in his lecture on the economics of taste last summer, the techno-economic sphere of society has already invaded the cultural enterprise of education. Education models itself on the pattern of corporate mentality. Administrators are not the intellectual leaders of the school, but the managers of a system. And teachers are not considered to have the inner authority of those who follow a calling in life, a vocation, but are considered to be staff. It is a short hop, skip, and jump from that situation into the replacement of staff by computers. The technological conception of education took over the schools quite some time ago. Moving in the devices cannot be seen as an innovation; rather, it brings a technical vision to completion. Computers would not have a place in schools had schools not already become possessed by the technical imagination.

How will computer programming eliminate curriculum in the schools?

Programming as a method of learning has entered the school through the introduction of what Papert calls "the LOGO environment." The aim of this computer environment is to replace curriculum. For example, currently, in schools, one of the subjects studied is English grammar; it is part of the curriculum. But grammar is not a subject that interests students very much; for most teachers, it is probably a pretty deadly subject to teach. The life has gone out of the subject. Because teachers themselves do not find life in such a subject, students find it totally unrelated to life. If teachers sensed the life of grammar they would certainly organize and demonstrate against the threat of having something they love removed from them. Teacher education courses have devised methods courses for the teaching of grammar, but with the concentration on method—in attempting to make the subject lively and interesting for the student, more and more life is drained from the thing itself. It is an instance of the now universal occurrence in which teachers themselves do not learn grammar and in so doing find the life within the things, but instead learn all kinds of techniques of infantilizing grammar to make it suitable to the psychology of the child. The attempt is to care for the child more than the thing, which is really a terrible kind of psychology because real learning is possible only by becoming the thing, not by turning the thing into a subjective child-centered psychological process.

Grammar has its own kind of life; it has a soul of its own. It has invisible spirits within it. Nouns, verbs, adjectives, adverbs, sentences, are extraordinary beings, full of character, personality, color, depth, imagination. And, they become even more interesting when they get together and shape a world, when they speak in unison, full of tension, vibrancy, resonance, each giving up a little of itself to make another word show hidden parts of itself. Of course, it takes a good deal of rote memorizing to learn the parts of speech and a good deal of diagramming to learn to see the dance of sentences. Such memorizing used to be called learning by heart; it is a learning through the heart. One learns by giving one's heart to the thing. We need a full psychology of grammar. It is tragic indeed that the focus is on the psychology of the child learning grammar. That psychology kills the thing. Grammar, of course, mightily resists such defilement, and in spite of all of the efforts of the methods courses, in fact perhaps because of them, grammar becomes increasingly difficult to learn, requiring a repetitious, detached, seemingly meaningless immersion in definitions, rules, and exercises, which can then be applied to actual writing. That is to say, the more concentration on method, the further the life of grammar recedes. The introduction of the computer takes this direction to its final conclusion by eliminating grammar altogether.

The LOGO approach to the teaching of grammar through computer programming is that grammar is not studied at all. Grammar is eliminated from the curriculum. The subject would be replaced by the programming of a general structure, for example, the structure of a poem, within which words are selected from a random list to fill in that structure. The student plays around inserting various words into the general structure until an error-free poem is produced—that is, one in which each part of grammar is correct. The aim is to bypass grammar because grammar is not interesting; but a child can feel like a poet by writing a poem, and, incidentally, effortlessly learns the parts of speech and what they do while constructing a poem.

The argument is in fact quite persuasive. When we learned to talk in our early years, none of us did so by studying vocabulary and the parts of speech. We would say something and perhaps be told that we had used an incorrect word or a word in the wrong place. Gradually, we learned to speak more or less correctly. Now, what is the difference between that kind of learning and the learning proposed here? Most obviously, learning how to talk occurs in the context of a family, a community, through the mediation of the breath and the heart of those with whom we are most intimately associated. Remove any such community or put them aside from the actual act of learning and into the role of cheerleaders and what do you have? I can best show the result by considering a poem generated by a thirteen-year-old girl, or, should we say, generated by a computer. This poem, reported and discussed by Seymour Papert, was produced by inserting words into a programmed structure one by one. The program would accept some words and reject others until the structure was filled out. If, for example, a noun was selected where the structure called for a verb, there would be some error message flashed on the screen and the student would try again. The error message, incidentally, would not be a judgment—in computer language there are no rights and wrongs, because, my heavens, we would not want the child to think badly about his performance! When an error message comes up—something like "that won't work, will it? Let's try again. I can't fit that word in here"—it is necessary to "debug" the program. At any rate, here is the thing produced by the child:

Insane Retard Makes Because Sweet Snoopy Screams

Sexy wolf lives thats why the sexy lady hates
Ugly man loves because ugly dog hates
Mad wolf hates because insane wolf skips
Sexy retard screams thats why the sexy retard
Hates
Thin snoopy runs because fat wolf hops
Sweet foginy skips a fat lady runs[4]

First, of course, this thing is not in any sense a poem, not even a failed poem. It is not that there is a lack of rhyme, rhythm, meter. None of that is really necessary for a poem. It is rather that this thing does not compel any attention. It has no life of its own. It has only the attention that anyone is willing to give it, and I have already given it far too much. Second, the words of the poem do not speak to each other to make anything that speaks. There is no internal tension between the words. It is a thing that imitates a poem but does not have the heart of a poem. However, the educationalist of programming might well agree that this is not a poem. The point, it would be argued, is that the child thinks that she is writing a poem; that makes her feel important, like an adult who is actually doing something meaningful. Actually, while she thinks she is writing poetry she is effortlessly, without thought, learning the parts of speech. Making something that looks like a poem is just the excuse for secretly teaching grammar without a grammar curriculum.

It is just here that the psychopathic character of programming as a method of learning begins to show its disguised ugliness, how education has gone from the order of the heart to the order of calculative manipulation. In order to highlight this psychopathy, it is necessary for a moment to describe this psychological illness in some detail. I am neither leaving the subject of computer learning nor imposing a psychological category onto programming, but rather describing the inherent psychology within programming as a method of learning.

Psychopathy is actually a kind of programming in life, learning how to debug life. The psychopath does everything effortlessly, freely, without any sense of inhibition, restraint, or suppression. Nothing of the world makes a claim on the soul of the psychopath. Cheating, lying, saying one thing and doing just the opposite without the least concern, changing a position from one moment to the next in order to satisfy the situation, the psychopath is always a winner. In appearing better than one actually is, successfully gliding along the surface, intelligently but without insight, without being emotionally moved, without feelings of the heart, only programmed feelings to suit the situation, psychopathy constantly assures that everything works smoothly, efficiently, always to one's advantage. Everything is a game—feelings, emotions, courtesy, love, sympathy for others, expressions of care. Like the little girl's poem, which looks like a poem but does not have the heart of a poem, the psychopath can imitate any form of behavior without it's going through the heart.

Look at the word *psychopath*—the pathos of soul. It is different from the word psychopathology, which is the logos of the suffering of the soul. Why is this illness called psychopathy? Because it describes the situation of the soul that is unaffected by anything. The psychopath lacks any erotic connections with the world. The illness is one of constant manipulation of one's own psychic processes for the satisfaction of the moment. The center of gravity is totally on the side of oneself. Is this not like the child who looks at the computer screen and sees there not a content, a curriculum that one must become in order to learn, but rather sees only his own psychological processes as they are happening each moment, and is given the task of manipulating them? Of course, it is fascinating, absolutely captivating to stare at oneself displayed on a screen for hours on end. Of course, it is intriguing to control one's own processes, making them do whatever is necessary to receive a result. Of course, this is exciting. But it has no heart.

This game of computer programming has nothing to do with content, with something that has a soul utterly different from our own in which learning involves learning to love the soul of that which we do not understand. The word *education* means a leading out of the soul; and that says learning consists of allowing our soul to enter, via the heart, into the things of the world, to mingle there in unfamiliar conversations, to be affected, moved by the soul of things, gradually learning to speak their language.

The roots of psychopathy are found in the loss of care for the things of the world. Learning by the method of programming concentrates on three components—the ego, the body, and an abstract sign on the computer screen. Seymour Papert names this sign a "turtle," which is no more than a kind of arrow on the screen that traces out geometric shapes according to computer commands. The programmer decides what he wants to construct, an operation of the ego, and relies on a vague memory of the body to determine how to move the arrow on the screen forward, backward, right, left, up and down. The object of computer learning is to remove the child from the actual world and to insert him into his own subjective processes where an imitation world is invented. A recent "Nova" television program devoted to the work of Seymour Papert provides a series of striking images of children learning to turn away from the world.

A first scene. A group of children stand out in an open field. The field is beautiful—tall green grass, purple and yellow flowers beneath a deep blue sky. The children are not playing in this field; in fact, they are quite oblivious to their wonderful surroundings. It is quite an extraordinary image. Imagine standing outside on a cool autumn morning; there is dew in the grass; the clouds play coy games, making themselves into shapes of monsters, old men with flowing white beards, beautiful princesses. The air, pure and cool, draws deep breaths. The coolness says that in a short time this grass will go to sleep for the winter; this may be the last time for long months to romp and play, turn somersaults. Even an adult could not resist being moved to play, or at the very least to walk and contemplate the change of seasons. But these children, unmoved by such beautiful things, walk off geometric shapes through the grass. One little girl is the turtle; her directions—ten steps forward, turn left, then another ten steps straight ahead, another left turn, ten more steps, and a final sharp left turn. The girl is blind to the world. And so are the rest of the children, who are all calculating the movements necessary to make a square. When they have completed the motions, they all go inside and sit in front of the computer and program the turtle on the screen to trace out the shape of a square. This scene is paradigmatic of computer learning. It is all an abstraction. Learning does not celebrate the actual things of the world, but turns away from the world in order to program an imitation world.

Another scene. Two small girls dressed in black leotards sit cross-legged on a stage, facing each other. Music starts. The girls spin around on their bottoms several times, rise from the floor, twirl several times past each other and then cartwheel back, crossing each other again. It is all perfectly executed. It looks like a dance. It is a perfect imitation of a dance. Yet, it is not a dance. Absolutely no tension shows on the faces of the girls, and there is no tension in their bodies, and no tension between their bodies, in the space between their movements. It is a perfect series of movements, but it is not interesting to watch. The viewer is not moved by the dance. There is no edge to it, no fearful, exciting feeling that the girls are right on the line between an earthly form, the natural movements of the body, and the transformation of the body into the world of the dance. The girls had programmed the entire sequence of movements on the computer, analyzing each movement necessary, and then followed this program to execute the motions. It is a new ballet—the dance of the psychopaths.

A third scene. A group of children are standing outside a building, evidently their school. They are crowded together watching a juggler. First he juggles four balls—red, green, yellow, blue. Then he juggles four pins. They fly through the air, not a one at rest. It is marvelous, magical. The children, however, are not delighted. How is it that they are not squealing, spellbound with such a wonder? The camera focuses on one little boy. His face is contorted with concentration. Eyes sharply focused, his head rapidly moves, following the motions of the balls and pins, carefully trying to dissect each movement of the juggler. The carnival is missed. The boy is already calculating the necessary commands to program the motions into the computer. Once done, he will program his body to carry out these same analyzed movements. He will be a perfect juggler, a psychopathic juggler.

Each of these portraits, along with our example of the girl's programmed poem, seems to be an instance of learning, each a rather remarkable accomplishment. And even if they lack that central dimension of heart, even if children are numbed, anesthetized to the world, are not the accomplishments the true measure of learning? Are not these children being prepared to enter the world fully capable of mastering any task quickly, efficiently, and perfectly? Is not the absence of heart that is so apparent in the actions of these children nothing more than a sentimental attachment to a world that no longer exists anyway? I can only answer by saying yes, indeed, this method of learning suits the culture we have constructed. The age of psychopathy is in its prime. But there are two reasons why this world, dominated by the technical imagination, is unacceptable, and must be reversed. Lurking within every psychopath is suicide, depression, and violence. Here is the price that we shall have to pay for quickly won perfection lacking the beauty of the heart. A massive bomb is in the making, and while we have made the bomb, it is our children who will explode it at the very moment when life, as it always does, gets its way, and manipulative calculation does not work. We see it already brewing in our children. The moment their calculations in life do not achieve the desired result, they are quick to violent anger.

The second reason is far more important. If, for a moment, it is possible to realize that education is really not for the sake of persons at all, but rather for the sake of the world, it suddenly becomes clear that child-centered learning is a preparation for the destruction of the world. Of course, we are filled with fears of the holocaust; the holocaust is already upon us. We shall be all dead before the bomb goes off.

I end with a final image. The film *Bladerunner* portrays the city of Los Angeles in the not-too-distant future. The image of that city ought to strike horror in our hearts. The city is in ruins. So much pollution fills the air that it is constantly raining. Most of the buildings are abandoned, as if some surge of overdevelopment by speculators did not bear fruit. Abandoned automobiles fill the streets. Garbage is scattered everywhere. Seamy characters roam the city. Everything is in utter ruin. Layered on top of this image lies a world of technological perfection. Automatic, air-lock doors open and close along the street. A huge dirigible passes over the city periodically, neon sign advertising some product. Police patrol the ruins in electronic airships. Lights, electronic gadgets, computers of every sort populate this city, a massive image of turning our back to the world in order to construct an imitation world. The main character of the film has the task of searching out a group of genetically engineered creatures who look exactly like human beings except that they are perfect—they are brilliant, have incredible athletic bodies, are extremely violent, seeing no reason whatsoever for refraining from killing anyone who blocks their psychopathic wishes.

My thought is simply this: How could it ever be that the world could matter so little that it becomes a garbage heap in the midst of incredible technical achievement? And, as I look at the beautiful, perfect, emotionless, heartless creatures, I fear that there is no need to develop genetic engineering to produce them. They may well be the product of public education.

Notes

1 Seymour Papert, *Mindstorms: Children, Computers, and Powerful Ideas* (New York: Basic Books, 1980), p. 8-9.

2 Ibid., p. 31.

3 Ibid., pp. 31-32.

4 Ibid., p. 49.

The Surrender of Control: Computer Literacy as Political Socialization of the Child

JOHN M. BROUGHTON
Teachers College, Columbia University

INSTRUMENTAL REASON

Hopefully, given the growing philosophical and political literacy around computers, it is no longer necessary to point out that the drive toward "computer literacy" represents a drive toward an upgraded version of *instrumental reason*. The embodiment of instrumental reason in computers was suggested originally by Horkheimer.[1] The application of the critique of instrumental reason to computer technology has since been extended by Weizenbaum.[2] The historical evolution of the instrumental world view in computer science and psychology has been documented by Dreyfus,[3] and its role in education examined by a host of commentators.[4]

Even Seymour Papert[5] acknowledges the specificity of the instrumental cognitive skill learned through programming. His work will be of particular concern in my discussion below. Currently, it appears to be serving a paradigmatic function in the field. Moreover, Papert himself is a highly qualified theoretical exponent, being relatively sophisticated in both philosophy and developmental psychology as well as artificial intelligence. Given his expertise and the broad appeal of his approach, I shall use several of his conceptions to illustrate how much more specific this instrumental skill is than he or his adherents have realised, and how the insidious nature and pervasive influence of instrumental reason has not yet been appreciated fully by the electronic learning movement.

In the process, it will be necessary to delineate the particular form that instrumental reason is taking in the community of educational computing and in the generation of "microkids" that it is spawning. The concept of instrumentality has not often been thought through carefully in the educational context, and a reexamination of its horizons may yield a clearer prospect. In the process, it will be necessary to reconsider what "ideology" is, and how it manifests itself in education.

VALUE-NEUTRALITY

While paying lip service to the specificity and limitations of programming rationality, even the sophisticated literature pertaining to computer literacy appears not to pause for much reflection on the matter. Rather, it tends to move on with the confidence that educational computing can be purified of the instrumental "bias," as though instrumental reason were some unfortunate contaminant to be filtered out and discarded. Behind this assumption lies the philosophically unrespectable but commonly accepted assumption of the "value-free" nature of technology: the computer is a neutral "tool" that can be used for either good or bad purposes. Papert, for example, phrases his version of this assumption in terms of a sharp distinction between "what computers can do and what society will choose to do with them."[6] It is particularly ironic that it is to the work of the progenitor of the concept of instrumental reason, Max Weber,[7] that the original conception of value-neutral truth has been attributed.[8]

But we have made some intellectual progress since then. The basic claim that truth is and needs to be value free is demonstrably incorrect, as is the fear that truth suffused with value commits us to the infinite regress of relativism.[9] High technology, too, is value laden. The computer *embodies* a certain kind of rationality; that rationality is the *condition of the possibility* of computer technology, its fundamental presupposition. Apparatuses and techniques do not occupy some privileged sphere sanitized of affective, moral, or political qualities. These qualities are not subjective infections to be eliminated with the right disinfectant, so that the purity of truth is left shining before us. Material products of human labor contain the policies through which they were intentionally constituted, whether those subjective purposes ever reach consciousness or not. The intentions and interests of producers have a structural, not a functional, relationship to the nature of their products. They are "constitutive" of that nature, rather than merely "affecting" or "influencing" aspects of the products. The process of constitution concretizes in the product ethical and political qualities as well as physical or technical ones. As philosophers from Hegel and Marx to Cassirer have argued, products are symbolic forms. The fact that the computer is a "symbolizer" par excellence should not be allowed to distract us from the fact that it is also a symbol. As such, to borrow Nelson Goodman's distinction, it serves not only the function of "denotating" but also that of "exemplifying."

The use of the noun "reason" in conjunction with the adjective "instrumental" may have had the misleading effect of suggesting that ideological distortion dwells only in the ideational sphere. It does not. In addition to "false consciousness," it inhabits falsified material reality and falsified practices. Ideology is not something residing solely in what we teach, but also in how we teach: what we teach with, what we teach through, and what we teach in, including the institutional structure, the methods, the techniques, the language, the relationship of expert to non-expert, and the instruments themselves. Instrumentation such as that provided by computer technology exemplifies a particular curricular and pedagogical orientation.

THE HIDDEN CURRICULUM

The elevation of "computer literacy" to prominence as a high priority educational objective hides the latent neopositivist curriculum of scientism. The implicit aim is a return to the traditional "hard" areas of intellectual endeavor. This is educational conservatism, but with a twist: back to the old basic skills—plus one metaskill. The hard areas are epitomized by those very same domains taken to have pioneered the invention of the microcomputer itself: natural science and mathematics. These are the realms where organized, logical, rule governed, algorithmic thinking are at a premium. Here, Piaget's theory is often invoked because of its claim that development moves naturally and inexorably toward the ultimate end point of systemic, logico-mathematical cognition.[10] The supposition (unsupported) that the discovery and perfection of the microcomputer was itself achieved by means of this kind of thinking serves only to confirm its preeminence. To borrow Papert's favored term, it is "space-age" thinking.

The epistemology associated with valorization of the traditional "hard" realms of abstract, experimental thought is one possessing an exclusive interest in objectivity, with the assumption that only knowledge has access to truth and that knowledge can be equated with thinking. The latter is construed narrowly as cognitive problem solving, where the "solutions" are arrived at by means of formal calculation, computation, and rational analysis, all of which are seen as types of information processing. The forms of inference considered legitimate are typically confined to induction and deduction, with abduction, interpretation, and other forms of conceptual construction being exiled from the realm. Such an orientation esteems the pragmatic virtues of cognitive order, organization, and systematicity, characterized by clarity, nonambiguity, nonredundancy, internal consistency, and noncontradiction—what we might call "programmatic lucidity."

This account of knowledge offers no challenge to the traditional positivist emphasis on discrete, objective *facts:* "Extended use of the computer as tutee can shift the focus of education from end product to process, from acquiring facts to manipulating and understanding them."[11] The conservative reduction of knowledge to factual units is revived by the dubious strategy of emphasizing the manipulability of these units; they lend themselves to incorporation into a sphere of personal possession and utility. The stress on "process" rather than "product" is used to convey an air of educational liberalism.

This approach comprises a functionalist updating of the traditional logical positivist epistemology, recast in the language of communications and information sciences. Thanks to the history of these sciences, which have grown up in close alignment with the "discipline" of organizations and management science, this recasting has brought with it an emphasis on knowledge as interacting "variables," mathematically defined "functions," "debugging procedures," hierarchical decision trees, abstract rule-structures, and networks of "modularizable" systems (to use Papert's term) governed by elaborately sequenced principles for recursive information flow and the continual upgrading of formal organizational structure. Elsewhere, I have called this modernized form of instrumental reason "systems positivism."[12] It is a rationalistic world view exhibiting all the characteristics identified as features of "administrative logic" by the critical social theorists of the Frankfurt School.

Thus, a significant feature of the hidden curriculum is instruction aimed at socializing individuals in the cognitive mode appropriate to functioning within bureaucratic organizations. The model is the child as an enterprising "manager," using "planning strategies" to organize people and information alike.[13] As sociologists from Max Weber to Talcott Parsons and Robert Merton have documented, preparation for this form of work involves a socialization into deference to a particular, functionally defined form of authority.[14] The concrete embodiment of this socialization in the school has been documented by researchers such as Kanter and Bernstein, and the process by which it takes psychological form has been charted in detail by Kohlberg.[15] The psychological end product of the socialization process is detailed empirically in the recent studies of female adulthood by Loevinger and of male adulthood by Levinson and Vaillant.[16]

THE INVISIBLE PEDAGOGY

Corresponding to the hidden curriculum and its implicit educational objectives is what Basil Bernstein has termed "invisible pedagogy."[17] The invisible pedagogy of the computerized curriculum is systems oriented. Like the hidden curriculum of computer literacy, its concealment is essential to its primary function of socialization. Its philosophy of mind as a formal, computational device, isomorphic with the computer, is embedded in an epistemology that emphasizes the active, constructive quality of thinking—"the child as builder" is Papert's phrase. The language employed to articulate this view of the participatory subject uses terms like "cognitive *operations*" and "programming *strategies*" to underline the active nature of the psychological processes involved.

It is on the basis of this active quality of thinking that Papert elevates programming far above computer assisted instruction: "In many schools today, the phrase 'computer-aided instruction' means making the computer teach the child. One might say the *computer is being used to program* the child. In my vision, *the child programs the computer.*"[18] And, "In the LOGO environment the relationship is reversed: The child, even at preschool ages, is in control: The child programs the computer."[19] The traditional teaching relationship is, indeed, reversed. The oedipal fantasy is finally realized: even the preschool child is "in control."[20] Children learn *by teaching*: "The child programs the computer. And in teaching the computer how to think, children embark on an exploration about how they themselves think."[21] The activity originates entirely within the child. In the language of psychologists, the child is the "locus of control." Since "development" is posited as cognitive development, which in turn is defined as active mastery, it is a small step to argue for programming as the best pedagogic tool for advancing the child's development as a whole.

COMPUTER LITERACY AS THE PROPAEDEUTIC SKILL

Before proceeding to unpack the social and political implications of Papert's kind of educational computing program, we would do well to note that theorists of this kind are no longer unaware of the critique of instrumental reason.[22] Typically, advocates of computer literacy in the schools, such as Papert, Kohl, and Galanter,[23] have a pluralist response to the critique, and I have heard a similar position presented by teachers in school settings where computing is a high priority. In order to bring to bear a political criticism of "computer literacy," it therefore is first necessary to clarify why the liberal acknowledgment of cognitive plurality is not able to silence objections to electronic learning.

The pluralist acknowledges that the skill learned through programming is only one of a number of alternative ways of thinking, but goes on to assert that it is an important and useful one, giving the child a vital experience of mastery. Furthermore, the argument goes, this logical skill has a broad range of transfer to other contexts and other thinking skills, and once mastered will lead children on to the discovery and mastery of other thinking skills. Programming logic provides a model of general problem-solving skills that are transferable to a wide range of other cognitive tasks. "Children can learn to use computers in a masterful way, and that learning to use computers can change the way they learn everything else."[24] Current claims of this kind are found throughout the writings of Papert, Minsky, Feurzeig, and their colleagues.[25]

It is worth noting that such a position contains a veritable web of ambiguity, suppressed premises, and misconceptions. First, it is mildly self-contradictory since it suggests that the choice of which skill to teach first, most, and best is relatively arbitrary, whereas the whole rationale for the priority of "computer literacy" in education is grounded on the centrality of programming logic, its function as the "leading edge" of mental development.[26]

Davy[27] has pointed out this insincerity in Papert's work. The proponents of the propaedeutic role of computer literacy behave in a manner that is grossly inconsistent with their espoused pluralism. They do not support their claims about the interconnectedness of different logics, or even display any interest in exploring them. They certainly do not encourage the children in their care to do so, nor do the latter appear to do so spontaneously, as Davy points out. Here, in educational technology, we see repeated the lesson of political history: pluralism in principle is a useful cover for hegemony in practice. Now that the era of empire has faded, the imperial tendency seeks its refuge in the last and least resistant zone of colonization—childhood.[28]

There is a second misconception smuggled in by the pluralist argument: the notion that instrumental reason is "a way of thinking." It is not. Rather, it presents itself as the definitive *rationality*, the exclusive and exhaustive principle of intelligent and objective understanding or action. It is an ideological world view embedded in a mystifying technology. It is pervasive and preemptive. It is even exhibited in the very rationale that we have just described, that teaching programming is instrumental to the learning of other things. Such appeals to utility and means-ends relations are used as primary justifications, without appeal to any rational grounding of the intrinsic value of programming skill or other ends to which it is a means. Whatever observations are marshaled in support of computing are also instrumentally conceived. For example, the motivation recruited by programming is an indirect one; children are not engaged by the intrinsic merits of programming, or by the joy of learning, but rather by the ulterior motive of satiating their own drives for mastery.[29]

This brings us to the third misconception: the assumption that children have a spontaneous interest in mastery. This assumption is unsupported in or by the literature on educational computing, and on closer examination it turns out to be simply untrue. It is an unfortunate assumption inherited from the unfortunate behaviorist movements in psychology and education, which were premised on the dubious mandate, passed down through the generations from Hobbes to Skinner, that "you have to control it (or yourself) before it controls you." Empirical research, if not rational reflection, reveals that meaning is of greater concern to children than mastery[30]—so much so that they would rather understand a situation than be rewarded in it.[31] Concealed in the prevalent appeals to the importance of experiences of mastery in the child's development is a chain of inference in which freedom is reduced to autonomy, autonomy is equated with independence, and independence is reduced to control—a series of conflations that does not stand up to even cursory scrutiny.[32]

Behind the equation of instrumental reason with cognitive style is a fundamental misunderstanding of *ideology*. Ideology is not just a set of beliefs, assumptions, or values. That view is the "ideology of ideology."[33] Rather, ideology is a mystifying mentality—a simulation of objectivity, a "false consciousness"—the very structure of which is distorted and distorting. Nevertheless, as Marx was quick to realise,[34] this does not imply that the systematically spurious is confined to the ideational level. False consciousness is inseparable from a self-deceptive way of life, the material instruments and methods in which that life-style is embodied, and the social relationships in terms of which it is conducted.[35] It is not one element in a natural repertoire of optional competencies. It is historically produced by societies under conditions of alienation and domination, forms of exploitation and suffering that it is designed to conceal. There is not a plurality of "ideologies." Ideology is singular—a kind of phenomenon, the fundamental and systematic falsification of knowledge and existence. As far as children are concerned, it is not enough to ask whether their development can be fostered by a critical awareness of ideology, because the very concept of development, as well as its methods, its experts, and the contexts in which it is regulated, is deeply ideological.[36]

This brings us to the fifth desideratum in the pluralist position. As demonstrated most cogently by Walkerdine and Sinha,[37] part of the ideological orientation implicit in the concept of development is the liberal assumption that education conveys *skills,* and that these skills are primarily *cognitive.* The approach to mind that preoccupies itself almost exclusively with cognition is the psychological component of the ideology of instrumental reason.[38] To speak pluralistically about computer use encouraging the use of other thinking skills is merely a recycling of this false presupposition. The role and significance of the cognitive in mental processes, in development, and in education has been vastly overestimated.[39]

Moreover, the primacy of conception over perception, or the cognitive over the aesthetic, is contradicted by both philosophical analysis and psychological research.[40] In addition to which, the notion that the formal, ordered, recursive logic of rule governed self-correcting systems is central to thinking is refuted by any careful examination of cognition in everyday experience[41] or in the educational process.[42] This applies a fortiori in the relationship between a person and a machine.[43] Paradoxically, artificial intelligence experts such as Winograd[44] have come to acknowledge that this kind of logic is not central even in artificially constrained "microworlds,"[45] and psychologists have come to admit that this is the case with experimental situations as well.[46]

There are further challenges to be borne in mind. The treatment of mental processes as transactions abstracted from agency and intentionality is of dubious validity.[47] Even the modern mentalist assumption that the mind traffics in representations has undergone serious reconsideration.[48] The assumption that mental processes are entirely or primarily "rule governed" is no longer undisputed.[49] In fact, some decades ago, Baldwin and Dewey, among others, demonstrated that even logic was not a matter of formal, abstract rules.[50] We should not allow the rhetoric of the "information revolution" to obscure the discovery that information itself is not central to mental processes.[51] The act of common or garden interpretation would be impossible if information were the medium in which it had to be conducted.[52] As pointed out by Searle,[53] even computers do not "process information"; they merely exhibit certain input-output relations.

Last but not least, we should note that the imperial term "computer literacy" has met its empirical Waterloo. Inherent in that term is the promise of generalizability comparable with the generativity of reading and writing. However, there is no evidence that programming skills transfer to other areas of psychological development, even cognitive ones. In fact, a recent comprehensive review of the literature by Pea and Kurland[54] suggests that virtually all the claims made about the beneficial educational effects of learning to program are not only inflated, but probably incorrect. The supposed "transfer" is more myth than reality. Moreover, Pea and Kurland reveal that there is not even support for the more parochial notion that learning to program aids children's mathematical thinking. Their own research study on transfer[55] revealed that Logo programming experiences had no effect on the planning skills that are deemed central to problem-solving skills. The tradition of grossly inflated claims identified in the artificial intelligence literature by Dreyfus[56] appears to have carried over into the research area of electronic learning.

These disconcerting conclusions would appear to confirm and extend the qualifications of an earlier review of pertinent literature of the 70s conducted by Ross and Howe.[57] Pea and Kurland's review appears to have already elicited considerable support from various quarters.[58] The contemporary stagnation of the once promising field of artificial intelligence[59] would appear to be paralleled by the psychological stagnation of the child whose cognitive development is based on programming: ontogeny recapitulates phylogeny. Hopefully, the deflationary impact of these findings will stimulate some reexamination of the semantic validity of that rather presumptuous phrase "computer literacy."

PROGRAMMING AND THE MASTERY OF THE COMPUTER

Having witnessed the considerable vulnerability of the pluralist retort to the critique of instrumental reason, let us return to the political subtext of computer literacy advocates like Papert. We examined above the systems-positivist understanding of development in such approaches: the view of mind as formal, procedural, and rule governed; the scientistic curricular objectives; and the pedagogy of the "active subject." The educational goal associated with such a philosophy of mind, epistemology, and theory of development is typically a *psychological* one. "The child programs the computer. And in teaching the computer how to think, children embark on an exploration about how they themselves think. The experience can be heady."[60] Children do not really learn how to think, they learn *how they think*.

Papert, recursively processing his days with Piaget, states that "thinking about thinking turns the child into an epistemologist."[61] This rather casual allusion to Piagetian theory embodies an exaggerated claim. Philosophical theorizing about knowledge is hardly reducible to someone thinking about his or her cognitive process,[62] however "heady" that experience might get. One cannot even assert with any confidence that thinking about thinking rather than thinking about something else amounts to turning the child into a psychologist. If it did, graduate training in psychology would be a total scam! There is a romantic "professionalization" of the child going on here that may belie the socialization function of "computer literacy."[63]

Papert's haste to dignify the child programmer with the status of a professional academic draws attention away from the fact that the child is simply engaged in business as usual. Educational Pragmatists have always told us that this was the natural way of developing: learning by doing and reflecting on it. According to Papert's own words, learning is simply turning tacit know-how into explicit know-that; intuitive knowledge becomes propositional knowledge. This may resemble the Socratic view, but it is actually the traditional Pragmatist way of explaining the development of intelligence out of action by reflective abstraction, as Woodward and Bernstein have documented.[64]

When advocacy for computer literacy starts with this vision of the child's relationship to the computer, it begs all the important questions. Concealed in the basic assertion that "in teaching the computer how to think, children embark on an exploration about how they themselves think" is a long chain of implicit assumptions: that computer operations are a form of "thinking"; that the computer does not "know" anything about how to "think" until programmed; that the child spontaneously wants to "teach" the computer; that the child's "mastery" entails that his or her input is entirely self-constructed; that the computer is receptive to whatever the child constructs and "teaches" it; that the content of the child's program becomes the form of the computer's "thinking"; that thinking about thinking as presented to the child by the computer is superior to thinking about thinking on his or her own or talking it over with someone else; and that what the child ends up constructing is not just a product of some of his or her own thinking but a more or less accurate model of all of his or her own thinking. Perhaps what is "heady" about the experience of child programmers is trying to cope with all these inferential leaps while maneuvering round the quotation marks at the same time.

This chain of dubious assumptions is by no means a Papertian idiosyncracy; it is a form of thought endemic to the computer culture. For example, a similar set of assumptions is to be found in the work of Minsky and Feurzeig.[65] A similar view of the active child is also endemic to mainstream developmental psychology, as in Piaget's theory, for example.[66] One is tempted to wonder, if this is the kind of loose, unsubstantiated, and presumptuous thinking that the computer experts have learned from all their experience of programming, what hope can we have for our microcomputing children?

Unexamined assumptions are characteristic of the unexamined life. In this sense, the computer communicates to children a way of actively pursuing cognitive control while actively fleeing examination of their lives.

COMPUTER LITERACY AND LIBERAL DEMOCRATIC VALUES

In the matrix of speculations underlying the vision of programming as education, the central themes are individualist, voluntarist, instrumental, utilitarian, idealist, and dualist. These qualities—characteristic features of the liberal, positivist tradition[67]—are interwoven here again and rearticulated by using the relationship between person and machine as both a metaphorical device and an opportunity to incorporate the prestige of advanced technology into the legitimization of traditional democratic values. It is worth spelling out the assumptive themes lying beneath this attempted resuscitation of liberal educational theory. It is notable how "defensive" these assumptions are, serving to narrow conceptual scope and restrict imagination of social and personal possibilities.[68]

Individualism. It is the individual child who is the absolute unit of analysis. The individual child is and should be only interested in his or her own thinking, not that of others. Like "reflective thinking," action takes only an individual form. Action is the pattern of movement overtly displayed by a biologically coherent, skin-bounded entity—it is the most mobile and useful capacity that the individual possesses. Collective action, such as that which produced computer technology and the idea of computer literacy, is ignored or denied. What is important for the functioning of democracy is that the *individual's* sphere of possession and control be expanded and stabilized.[69] It is the acquisition of methods by the individual that defines his or her viability in the career structure of the modern socioeconomic world.[70]

Voluntarism. Once the primacy of the possessive individual is accepted, it seems only sensible to suppose that it is the individual child who is the source and principle of action. The child is always the "embarker," the computer only the carrier. Despite the claim that the computer's processing is a valid model of the child's thought, and the claim that thought is intrinsically active (since it is derived from action), the activity of the computer is denied. The underlying conception of action is linear and Newtonian, strangely at odds with the recursive logic of computing. If the child programs the computer, that's that: the child is cause, the computer, mere effect. The possibility of actively subordinating or exposing oneself to controlling surveillance through activity is eliminated. The possibility of controlling through appearing passive, such as in passive aggression, is also precluded.[71] Moreover, the fact that choosing one kind of action always entails rejecting others is not acknowledged.

Instrumentalism. Often, this posing of the computer as inert is facilitated by playing down the structural and functional complexity of the computer, by referring to it as a "tool."[72] High technology is reduced to the simple enumeration of its particular products. Correlatively, the possibilities of the child's actions are reduced to instrumental ones comparable to tool use. This view is often supported by sociobiological appeals to tool use as the definitive feature of *Homo sapiens*.[73]

Utilitarianism. The relationship of child to computer is thereby construed as one of active to passive, and such a relationship necessarily implies mastery of the latter by the former. The computer has only greater or lesser utility—it has no value in itself. It is the purposes to which the tool is put that define the value of the action. Morality is reduced to objective utility, and computer technology is exonerated of any responsibility.

Idealism. This construction of the relationship as absolutely asymmetrical, with value only being imposed upon the instrument, is idealist, because it attributes to mental constructions the exclusive capacity to make meaning. Meaning can only reside in what sense we make of the material world.[74] The material world can make nothing of us, and it cannot embody meaning. Consequently, we can only project meaning onto the inert substance of objective nature. We cannot find meaning *in* its objects.

Dualism. Idealism presupposes a subject-object dualism. Subjectivity resides in the individual mind, objectivity, in the external, observable world. The possibility that one labors to find oneself objectified in one's creations, and the possibility that one can discover other subjectivities through their creative expressions, are precluded. The possibility that the intentional world of the producers of the computer is communicated to the consumers via the computer is rendered inconceivable. After all, only instrumental action is possible, not expressive or interpretive action. The notion that the computer could mediate authority or power by representing it becomes unimaginable.

THE CHILD AS ORGANIC MACHINE

There is an alternative way to interpret the enterprise of programming-based computer literacy. This interpretation starts from the assumption that children have not yet attained the full autonomy of free citizens of a democracy. As a result, children experience as mastery what is actually a subordination of their mental processes and hence themselves to the epistemic presuppositions built into the particular computational form of the devices themselves—the fact that they can only process information, and the fact that they require their input to take a single logical form.

The strange ambiguity of control is transparent in the following statement from one of the major texts in the field of electronic learning: "To use the computer as *tutee* is to tutor the computer; for that, the student or teacher doing the tutoring must learn to program, *to talk to the computer in a language it understands*."[75] The dialectic of control is one in which the interlocutor who is more desperately compelled by the need for control will allow himself or herself to be constrained rigidly by the other if that constraint serves as a means to an eventual sense of mastery.

According to this critical interpretation, in the Logo program, for example, children are first systematically misled into thinking that mind is separate from and dominates body (the experience is "head-y"). Next, they are further misled into assuming that thought is the dominant quality of the mind. Finally, in the coup de grace, they are encouraged to mistake the form of the computational logic of the device for a valid model of their own thinking. Certainly, these children, if they develop into psychologists or epistemologists, are likely to promote the degenerate theoretical conception of the human being as a self-propelling information processor.

What is a useful assumption for ambitious artificial intelligence experts who want to explain psychological processes through simulation[76] is passed off to the child as a necessary precept of computer literacy. When Papert talks of "forging new relationships between computers and people,"[77] he is perhaps unaware that one way in which he has already done this is by just such a sleight of hand. I do not mean to imply that Papert, Minsky, et al. are coconspirators, or that any intentional deceit has taken place. On the contrary, the magical displacement of subject by object just described is a regular feature of any idealist position. Idealism pivots on precisely this conjuring trick: a displacing of the subject by the object by encouraging the subject to assume that the object as it presents itself is a full and valid objectification of the subjective. It is the "tragedy of culture" identified and described so compassionately by Georg Simmel[78]—a "misrecognition" of ourselves. We are willingly misled insofar as we assume that our minds exhaustively construct the meaning of whatever material reality is the object of our experience.[79]

According to the more critical perspective suggested here, the conjunction of computer function and mental function, mediated by the concept of active mastery, is itself a control mechanism. The goal of this "new relationship" is to foster the primacy of computational procedures to such a degree that the computer's influence over the child takes on the power of "action at a distance." Papert, for example, advocates "ways in which the computer presence could contribute to mental processes not only instrumentally but in more essential, conceptual ways, influencing how people think even when they are far removed from physical contact with the computer."[80]

The push for computerization of education and psychology represents an admission that authority cannot be imposed directly upon individuals by society but instead requires psychological mediation. As critical philosophers, sociologists, and historians such as Horkheimer, Adorno, Foucault, and Lasch have documented,[81] power is not the suppression of natural qualities or the imposition of artificial ones. It is the enthusiastic collusion of the individual in a process whereby he or she participates in producing, consuming, and privatizing precisely those forms of thinking and being that are most conducive to advances in the regulation of public life. In Logo, we see the production, consumption, and privatization of mastery in a form modeled on the control already implicit in the hidden curriculum and invisible pedagogy of microelectronic technology.

In his book, Papert celebrates the way in which computing microworlds so effectively solicit the collusion of the child. The choice is unforced. "I have invented ways to take educational advantage of the opportunities to master the art of *deliberately* thinking like a computer."[82] The ethical status of his endeavor hinges on the "freedom" with which it endows the child—the freedom to be deliberate without having to deliberate. Is this emancipatory education, or just "taking advantage of the opportunities"? Perhaps it is the merger of the two that appeals. In the morphology of the computer "nut," the outer shell of liberation protects the tender kernel of control—a dialectical reconciliation indeed, and a hard one to crack.

Moreover, Papert claims that "by deliberately learning to imitate mechanical thinking, the learner becomes able to articulate what mechanical thinking is and what it is not."[83] Politely passing over the fact that what computing is *not* receives almost no consideration at all, let us remark that it is precisely this distinction between mechanical and nonmechanical that is blurred in the abstract computing context where it is systems ideology that provides the possibilities of choice and the contours of movement. Is an organized program "mechanical" or not? "Organizing" seems to be the opposite of "mechanizing," playing as it does upon the apparent antonymy of organism and mechanism, animal and machine. Psychological organization must therefore be the epitome of liberation, displacing as it does that rigidity of mind that ties us down to the mere object world. Let us at least be animals!

The concept of "organization" serves to biologize rationality and merge the mechanical with the human. To account for its mediation by the psychological world, instrumental reason needs an ontology that recasts the relations between the physical, vital, and human domains. It is through the systemic, bodily metaphor of the smoothly functioning organ that this is achieved. Positivism becomes systems positivism. The metaphor is used to create the illusion that, in organization, the rigid automatisms of the mere machine have been transcended.

But rather than leaving the mechanical behind, the systems approach manages to produce a new continuity between organization and mechanization. This merger allows a powerful rationalization of the latter through the former; the mechanical is raised to a new power. The embodiment of the continuum in the form of computers allows their programmers to become more fully rationalized as their universe of action and thought is created in the image of the organic machine. The Trojan horse lives on.

THE CONTROL OF EDUCATION

Implicit in the microelectronic technology of computers is a particular form of education and a specific set of educational objectives. This educational package only appears to be a "program," to be used or dispensed with at will. In fact, under the surface of the computing device, it is wired in as surely as are the microchips, formatted into the actual disks, motivated by the actual drives. It is a function of the very *microelectronicity* of the computer, carrying all of the thickness of connotation acquired through word and deed over the centuries by the physical, mathematical, and engineering sciences. This meaning embraces all of their mechanical and electrical inventions, their various economic and political achievements, and the manifold of cultural symbolism invested in technical instrumentation and labor-saving devices.

We are used to talking about "educational software." The attempt at predetermining educational practices is only partially concealed by the dualism of "hardware" and "software." The hardware is educational too. All the talk of flexibility and adaptability of computer use is a thin disguise for the underlying rigidity of curricular and pedagogical practices presupposed by the particular form that this technology, by our design, has taken. The scientific and technological choices made and the paths not taken are condensed into this single, highly expressive object. The computer exemplifies a particular vision of civilization, past as well as future.

Technology is not just products or "tools." It is *practices.* Practices have the potential to incorporate other practices. Some practices adjust to becoming part of another whole. At present, the practice of education would appear to be engaged in a willing symbolic subordination of itself to the practice of technology. Papert states with confidence: "Schools as we know them today will have no place in the future. But it is an open question whether they will adapt by transforming themselves into something new or wither away and be replaced."[84] The imperative for transformation is experienced as extrinsic, as impinging upon and making demands of the educational system. Education faces the forced choice of either surviving by adjustment to reality, or risking the withering look of the computer technocracy.

Policies of economic, political, and military advance through the incubation and delivery of emergent technologies require corresponding emergent educational objectives to serve not only as the instrument of their popularization but also as the symbolic form of their recognition. High technology cannot maintain the courage of its conviction unless it is awarded high priority throughout the social and cultural system, and so come to seem inevitable. The cultural life of advanced societies pivots on the symbolic consistency of this relation of synecdoche, the fidelity of part to whole.

Educational practice is not passively co-opted. It enthusiastically participates, actively "adapting" to reality and seeing itself in turn represented in the majestic progress of civilization. Its self-esteem, markedly lower than most professions, is correspondingly repaired. But the promising, restorative features of finding a more meaningful location in the social whole tend to turn into a perverse and obsequious form. This occurs to the extent that the cultural pervasiveness of ideology goes undetected, when the confinement of rationality to a particular technical form is confused with the development of reason as a universal ideal. The consequence of such a conflation is that the instrumentality of our arrangement with technology goes unnoticed. Our identification with the computer is so convincing that we are unable to see that we are allowing education to be used as a means to the end of technological progress. We fail to notice that our dedication to a "systems" perspective commits us to the inevitable homogenizing and hierarchizing mandate that that perspective incorporates.

CONCLUSION

"Suffer the little children to come unto me." Culturally, we have constructed a synecdoche in the liaison between our children and our computers. This icon of the little leading the big is a part standing for the whole of the current history of education. In our haste to preserve a species whose survival is increasingly threatened, we have made a premature marriage between a fairy tale prince and a child bride. What is the symbolism of sending the child to lead the technological revolution but an oblique reference to our own sense of diminution and vulnerability? What is the symbolism of confronting that child with the full force of technological mastery but a disguising of our own aggression toward that weak and helpless self? After all, we know that progress is never achieved without sacrifice.

Innocence, promise, power, and surrender are the watchwords of this modern secular eschatology.

POSTSCRIPT: FREUD AND CASSANDRA

After a recent talk in which I had given my usual jaundiced perspective on the computer revolution, a friendly colleague came up to me and said, simply: "Don't you like the fruit of man's invention? Don't you like trains, planes, and telephones? If not, why do you use them?" For a moment I felt like the vegetarian caught in leather boots, or the grow-your-own hippy found eating out of a can. Then I recalled a story from the Viennese annals.

Freud's son once went on a long journey, and spurred on by a great desire to speak to him, Freud confronted the telephone for the very first time. "What a marvellous invention to allow one to speak to someone so far away!" he is reported to have said immediately afterwards. Then he thought for a moment and added, "But if it hadn't been for the invention of the locomotive, my son would never have been able to go so far away!"

Prophets of doom fare no better than the bearers of bad news. No one wants to behold the tragic countenance of a Cassandra. But after all, as many a chagrined Trojan later recalled, Cassandra was right: the Greeks really were folks to beware of. When she cast a jaundiced eye on their gift, it wasn't just because she didn't like horses.

Notes

I am grateful to the following for their various contributions: Michael Black, Stephen Brookfield, Paul Chevigny, Colette Daiute, Margaret Honey, Richard Kitchener, Dene Leopold, Jack Mezirow, Roy Pea, Edmund Sullivan, and a teacher whose name is Tom. I am also grateful to have had the opportunity of participating in a study group on "high teachnology" with Maxine Greene, Joan Gussow, Steven Kerr, Robert McClintock, Douglas Sloan, Jonas Soltis, and several other colleagues, in a rare collective endeavor that was sponsored and encouraged by Michael Timpane. To Marta Zahaykevich, I feel a special gratitude: her sympathetic understanding of high technology has softened its impact upon me and ameliorated my more irrational fears.

1 M. Horkheimer, "The Concept of Man," in *The Critique of Instrumental Reason* (New York: Seabury Press, 1974).

2 J. Weizenbaum, *Computer Power and Human Reason* (San Francisco: W. H. Freeman, 1976).

3 H. L. Dreyfus, *What Computers Can't Do* (New York: Harper & Row, 1979).

4 For some examples, see M. Greene, "Philosophy Looks at Microcomputers," *Computers in the Schools* 1, no. 3 (1985): 3-11; E. V. Sullivan, "Computers, Culture and Educational Futures: A Critical, Reflective Mediation on Papert's 'Mindstorms,'" (Toronto: Strategic Planning Documents on Computers and Education, Ontario Ministry of Education, 1983); H. Ginsburg, "Computers for Little Children?" (Paper presented at the Kenan Convocation, Chapel Hill, N.C., 2 June 1984); M. Streibel, "An Analysis of the Theoretical Foundations for the Use of Microcomputers in Early Childhood Education" (Paper presented at the annual meeting of the American Educational Research Association, New Orleans, April 1984); J. M. Broughton, "Psychosocial Aspects of Computers in Education" (Paper presented at the American Educational Research Association, New Orleans, April 1984).

In this book, see the following articles: D. Sloan, "On Raising Critical Questions about the Computer in Education," 1-9; and J. Davy, "Mindstorms in the Lamplight."

5 S. Papert, *Mindstorms: Children, Computers, and Powerful Ideas* (New York: Basic Books, 1980).

6 Ibid., p. 6.

7 M. Weber, "'Objectivity' in Social Science and Social Policy," in *The Methodology of the Social Sciences*, ed. E. A. Shils and H. A. Finch (Glencoe, Ill.: The Free Press, 1949).

8 T. Parsons, "Value-Freedom and Objectivity," in *Max Weber and Sociology Today*, ed. O. Stammer (New York: Harper & Row, 1971). See also the reinterpretation of Weber's and Parsons's

positions in J. Habermas, "Discussion," also in *Max Weber and Sociology Today;* and the commentary on all three papers in F. R. Dallmayr and T. A. McCarthy, eds., *Understanding and Social Inquiry* (Notre Dame, Ind.: University of Notre Dame Press, 1977).

9 F. Cunningham, *Objectivity in Social Science* (Toronto: University of Toronto Press, 1973); J. Habermas, *Knowledge and Human Interests* (Boston: Beacon Press, 1971); K.-O. Apel, "Normative Ethics and Strategical Rationality," *Graduate Faculty Philosophy Journal* 9, no. 1 (1982): 81–108; and B. Fay, *Social Theory and Political Practice* (London: George Allen & Unwin, 1975).

10 B. Inhelder and J. Piaget, *The Growth of Logical Thinking from Childhood to Adolescence* (New York: Basic Books, 1958). See also J. M. Broughton, "Piaget's Structural Developmental Psychology, II: Logic and Psychology," *Human Development* 24, no. 3 (1981): 195–224, and "Not Beyond Formal Operations, but Beyond Piaget," in *Beyond Formal Operations,* ed. M. Commons, F. Richards, and C. Armon (New York: Praeger, 1984).

11 R. P. Taylor, Introduction to *The Computer in the School: Tutor, Tool, Tutee,* ed. R. P. Taylor (New York: Teachers College Press, 1980).

12 J. M. Broughton and M. K. Zahaykevich, "The Peace Movement Threat," *Teachers College Record* 84, no. 1 (1982):152–173; and J. M. Broughton, "The Psychological Origins of Nuclear War," *Forum International* 3 (1983): 163–187. This account of the emergence of cybernetic neopositivism draws heavily on J. Habermas, "Dogmatism, Reason and Decision: On Theory and Praxis in Our Scientific Civilization," in *Theory and Practice* (London: Heinemann, 1974), and *Legitimation Crisis* (Boston: Beacon Press, 1975).

13 On planning strategies, see D. Forbes and M. Greenberg, *Children's Planning Strategies* (San Francisco: Jossey-Bass, 1982). For a graphic example of how the enterprising child manager comes to manipulate people in the environment as though they were informational variables, see H. Kohl, "Should I Buy My Child a Computer?" *Harvard Magazine* (September–October 1982): 14–21.

14 For a recent summary and restatement of this position from a critical perspective, see R. Sennett, *Authority* (New York: Vintage Books, 1980).

15 R. M. Kanter, "The Organization Child: Experience Management in a Nursery School," *Sociology of Education* 45, no. 2 (1972): 186–212; B. Bernstein, *Class, Codes and Control* (London: Routledge & Kegan Paul, 1975); L. Kohlberg, C. Levine, and R. Hewer, *Moral Stages: A Current Formulation and a Response to Critics* (Basel, Switz.: Karger, 1983); L. Kohlberg, *Essays on Moral Development,* vol. 2, *The Psychology of Moral Development* (New York: Harper & Row, in press).

16 J. Loevinger and R. Wessler, *Measuring Ego Development* (San Francisco: Jossey-Bass, 1970); D. J. Levinson, *Seasons of a Man's Life* (New York: Ballantine, 1978); G. Vaillant, *Adaptation to Life* (Boston: Little, Brown, 1977).

17 B. Bernstein, "Class and Pedagogies, Visible and Invisible," in *Class, Codes and Control,* vol. 3 (London: Routledge & Kegan Paul, 1975).

18 Papert, *Mindstorms,* p. 5 (emphasis in original).

19 Ibid., p. 19.

20 The extent to which the child actually displaces the adult, and the pleasure that accompanies this aspect of computing is reported by both Kohl ("Should I Buy My Child a Computer?") and Ginsburg ("Computers for Little Children?").

21 Papert, *Mindstorms,* p. 19.

22 Davy, "Mindstorms in the Lamplight," (in this book).

23 Papert, *Mindstorms;* Kohl, "Should I Buy My Child a Computer?"; E. Galanter, "Homing in on Computers," *Psychology Today* (September 1984): 30–33, and *Kids and Computers: The Parents' Microcomputer Handbook* (New York: Putnam, 1983).

24 Papert, *Mindstorms,* p. 8.

25 W. Feurzeig, S. Papert, M. Bloom, R. Grant, and C. Solomon, *Programming Languages as a Conceptual Framework for Teaching Mathematics,* Report No. 1899 (Cambridge, Mass.: Bolt,

Beranek & Newman, 1969); M. Minsky, "Form and Content in Computer Science," *Communications of the ACM* 17 (1970): 197–215; S. Papert, "Teaching Children Thinking," *Programmed Learning and Educational Technology* 9 (1972): 245–255; S. Papert, "Teaching Children to be Mathematicians Versus Teaching About Mathematics," *International Journal of Mathematical Education, Science and Technology* 3 (1972): 249–262; I. Goldstein and S. Papert, "Artificial Intelligence, Language and the Study of Knowledge," *Cognitive Science* 1 (1977): 84–123; W. Feurzeig, P. Horwitz, and R. S. Nickerson, *Microcomputers in Education* Report No. 4798 to Department of Health, Education and Welfare (Cambridge, Mass.: Bolt, Beranek & Newman, 1981).

26 Streibel, "An Analysis of the Theoretical Foundations for the Use of Microcomputers in Early Childhood Education."

27 Davy, "Mindstorms in the Lamplight," (in this book).

28 On the labile and displaceable nature of "colonization," see A. Memmi, *The Colonizer and the Colonized* (Boston: Beacon Press, 1968). On the colonization of the child, see J. J. Voneche, "Victor, Marguerite and Armande, Jacqueline, Laurent and Lucienne, or the Difficulty of Growing Up in French-Speaking Countries," in *Critical Theories of Psychological Development*, ed. J. M. Broughton (New York: Plenum, 1985).

29 A related criticism is offered by Ginsburg in "Computers for Little Children?" Of course, if learning were to be equated with mastery, then this last objection of mine would seem superfluous. Such an equation appears to have been made surreptitiously via the notion that learning is a form of "competence" or a set of "competencies." However, I know of no convincing argument that knowledge or any other legitimate educational objective can be reduced to a matter of control. Far from it, there are very convincing reasons to distinguish and contrast the two (M. Young, ed., *Knowledge and Control* [London: Collier Macmillan, 1971]). The interpretation of education as "competency-based learning" is subject to the same critical treatment (C. A. Bowers, "Emergent Ideological Characteristics of Educational Policy," *Teachers College Record* 79, no. 1 [1977]. 34–54; D. Huebner, "Curriculum Language and Classroom Meanings," in *Curriculum Theorizing*, ed. W. F. Pinar [Berkeley: McCutchan, 1975]). Finally, I might note that in the above discussion I have ducked the issue of the relationship between learning and *development*, an important and difficult question (H. Furth, *Piaget and Knowledge* [Englewood Cliffs, N.J.: Prentice-Hall, 1969]; L. Kohlberg and R. Mayer, "Development as the Aim of Education," *Harvard Educational Review* 42 [1972]: 449–496; D. Kuhn, "Mechanisms of Cognitive and Social Development: One Psychology or Two?" *Human Development* 21 [1978]: 92–118).

30 J. Piaget, "Piaget's Theory," in *Handbook of Child Psychology*, 4th ed., vol. 1, ed. P. H. Mussen (New York: John Wiley, 1983); L. Kohlberg, "Early Education: A Cognitive Developmental View," *Child Development* 39 (1968): 1013–1062.

31 L. Kohlberg, "Stage and Sequence," in *Handbook of Socialization Theory and Research*, ed. D. Goslin (Chicago: Rand McNally, 1969).

32 P. London, *Behavior Control* (New York: Harper & Row, 1969); N. Chomsky, "Psychology and Ideology," *Cognition* 1, no. 1 (1972): 11–46; Habermas, *Legitimation Crisis*.

33 J. M. Broughton, "Review of Joseph Gabel's 'False Consciousness,'" *Telos* 29 (1976): 223–235.

34 K. Marx, *Capital*, vol. 1, ed. F. Engels (New York: International Publishers, 1967). See also R. Lichtman, "Marx's Theory of Ideology," *Socialist Revolution* 23 (1975): 45–76.

35 J. Gabel, *False Consciousness* (London: Basil Blackwell, 1975).

36 D. Ingleby, "The Psychology of Child Psychology," in *The Integration of the Child into the Social World*, ed. M. P. M. Richards (Cambridge: Cambridge University Press, 1974); J. M. Broughton, "Dialectics and Moral Development Ideology," in *Readings in Moral Education*, ed. P. Scharf (Minneapolis: Winston, 1978); and "Piaget's Structural Developmental Psychology, V: Ideology-Critique and the Possibility of a Critical Developmental Psychology," *Human Development* 24, no. 6 (1981): 382–411; Broughton, ed., *Critical Theories of Psychological Development*.

37 V. Walkerdine and C. Sinha, "The Internal Triangle: Language, Reasoning and the Social Context," in *The Social Context of Language,* ed. I. Markova (New York: John Wiley, 1978); V. Walkerdine, "From Context to Text: a Psychosemiotic Approach to Abstract Thought," in *Children Thinking Through Language,* ed. M. Beveridge (London: Edward Arnold, 1982).

38 E. E. Sampson, "Cognitive Psychology as Ideology," *American Psychologist* 36 (1981): 730-743. See also J. M. Broughton, "The History, Psychology and Ideology of the Self," in *Psychology and Ideology,* ed. K. Larsen (Norwood, N.J.: Ablex, 1985).

39 J. Macmurray, *Reason and Emotion* (London: Faber & Faber, 1935); Dreyfus, *What Computers Can't Do;* R. B. Zajonc, "Feeling and Thinking: Preferences Need No Inferences," *American Psychologist* 35 (1980): 151-175; Sloan, "On Raising Critical Questions about the Computer in Education," (in this book).

40 M. Merleau-Ponty, *The Primacy of Perception* (Evanston, Ill.: Northwestern University Press, 1964); Symposium on J. J. Gibson and Perception, *Synthese* 18 (1967); P. Tibbets, ed., *Perception: Selected Readings in Science and Phenomenology* (Chicago: Quadrangle Books, 1969).

41 M. Merleau-Ponty, *The Structure of Behavior* (Boston: Beacon Press, 1963); U. Neisser, *Cognition and Reality* (San Francisco: W. H. Freeman, 1976); P. Ricoeur, *Interpretation Theory: Discourse and the Surplus of Meaning* (Fort Worth: Texas Christian University Press, 1976); J. M. Broughton, "Not Beyond Formal Operations, but Beyond Piaget."

42 Streibel, "An Analysis of the Theoretical Foundations for the Use of Microcomputers in Early Childhood Education."

43 D. Ihde, "A Phenomenology of Man-Machine Relations," in *Work, Technology and Education,* ed. W. Feinberg and H. Rosemont (Urbana, Ill.: University of Illinois Press, 1975); J. Soltis, "Computers, Tools and Schools" (Paper presented at the Faculty Conference on Emerging Technologies, Teachers College, Columbia University, 25 February 1983).

44 T. Winograd, "What Does It Mean to Understand Language?" *Cognitive Science* 4 (1980): 209-241.

45 Dreyfus, *What Computers Can't Do.*

46 A. Giorgi, "The Experience of the Subject as a Source of Data in a Psychological Experiment," *Review of Existential Psychology and Psychiatry* 7 (1967): 169-176; Neisser, *Cognition and Reality.*

47 J. R. Searle, *Intentionality* (New York: Cambridge University Press, 1983); E. V. Sullivan, *Critical Psychology* (New York: Plenum, 1984); H. L. Dreyfus, *Husserl, Intentionality and Cognitive Science* (Cambridge: MIT Press, 1982).

48 Dreyfus, *What Computers Can't Do.* See also S. Hook, *Language and Philosophy* (New York: New York University Press, 1969); D. Dennett, *Brainstorms: Philosophical Essays on Mind and Psychology* (Montgomery, Vt.: Bradford Books, 1978); C. Taylor, "Consciousness," in *Explaining Human Behavior,* ed. P. F. Secord (Beverly Hills, Calif.: Sage, 1982). The various critics of representationalism draw on the philosophical traditions of Wittgenstein, Heidegger, and Polanyi, among others.

49 D. Ingleby, "New Paradigms for Old," *Radical Philosophy* 6 (1973): 42-46.

In this book, see the following article: H. L. Dreyfus and S. E. Dreyfus, "Putting Computers in Their Proper Place: Analysis versus Intuition in the Classroom," 40-63.

50 J. M. Baldwin, *Thought and Things,* 3 vols. (London: Swan Sonnenschein, 1906-1911); J. Dewey, *Logic: The Theory of Inquiry* (New York: Holt, Rinehart & Winston, 1938). See also J. M. Broughton and D. J. Freeman-Moir, eds., *The Cognitive Developmental Psychology of James Mark Baldwin* (Norwood, N.J.: Ablex, 1982).

51 R. DeVries and L. Kohlberg, "Relations Between Piaget and Psychometric Assessments of Intelligence," in *Current Topics in Early Childhood Education,* ed. L. Katz (Norwood, N.J.: Ablex, 1977). See also D. Elkind, "Conservation and Concept Formation," in *Studies in Cognitive Development,* ed. D. Elkind and J. H. Flavell (New York: Oxford University Press, 1969); and D. W. Hamlyn, "The Concept of Information in Gibson's Theory of Perception," *Journal of the Theory of Social Behavior* 6 (1974); 1-17.

52 C. Taylor, "Interpretation and the Sciences of Man," *Review Of Metaphysics* 25 (1971): 1-51; Winograd, "What Does It Mean to Understand Language?"

53 J. R. Searle, "Minds, Brains and Programs," *Behavioral and Brain Sciences* 3 (1980): 353-373.

54 R. D. Pea and D. M. Kurland. "On the Cognitive Effects of Learning Computer Programming," *New Ideas in Psychology* 2, no. 2 (1984): 137-168.

55 R. D. Pea and D. M. Kurland, *Logo Programming and the Development of Planning Skills,* Technical Report No. 16 (New York: Center for Children and Technology, Bank Street College of Education, 1983).

56 Dreyfus, *What Computers Can't Do.*

57 P. Ross and J. Howe, "Teaching Mathematics Through Programming: Ten Years On," in *Computers in Education,* ed. R. Lewis and D. Tagg (Amsterdam: North-Holland, 1981).

58 G. Salomon, "On Ability Development and Far Transfer," *New Ideas in Psychology* 2, no. 2 (1984): 169-174; E. V. Sullivan, "On the Cognitive and Educational Benefits of Teaching Children Programming," *New Ideas in Psychology* 2, no. 2 (1984): 175-179; L. Schauble, "The Feasibility of a Developmental Cognitive Science," *New Ideas in Psychology* 2, no. 2 (1984): 181-183.

59 Dreyfus and Dreyfus, "Putting Computers in Their Proper Place: Analysis versus Intuition in the Classroom," (in this book).

60 Papert, *Mindstorms,* p. 19.

61 Ibid.

62 A. Blasi and E. C. Hoeffel, "Adolescence and Formal Operations," *Human Development* 17, no. 5 (1974): 344-363; J. M. Broughton, "'Beyond Formal Operations': Theoretical Thought in Adolescence," *Teachers College Record* 79, no. 1 (1977): 87-98.

63 C. Lasch, "Chip of Fools: Review of S. Turkle's 'The Second Self' and J. D. Bolter's 'Turing's Man,'" *The New Republic,* 13-20 August 1984, 25-28.

64 W. R. Woodward, "Young Piaget Revisited: From the Grasp of Consciousness to Decalage," *Genetic Psychology Monographs* 99 (1979): 131-161; R. Bernstein, *Praxis and Action* (Philadelphia: University of Pennsylvania Press, 1971).

65 M. Minsky, "I Think Therefore I Am," *Psychology Today,* April 1969, 30-32; Feurzeig et al., *Programming Languages as a Conceptual Framework for Teaching Mathematics.*

66 J. M. Broughton, "Piaget's Structural Developmental Psychology, III: Function and Knowledge," *Human Development* 24, no. 4, (1981): 257-285.

67 D. Manning, *Liberalism* (New York: St. Martin's Press, 1976).

68 J. M. Broughton, "The Genesis of Moral Domination," in *Lawrence Kohlberg's Theory of Moral Development: For and Against,* ed. S. Modgil and C. Modgil (Brighton, Eng.: Falmer, 1985).

69 C. B. MacPherson, *The Political Theory of Possessive Individualism* (New York: Oxford University Press, 1962).

70 D. Riesman, N. Glazer, and R. Denney, *The Lonely Crowd* (New Haven: Yale University Press, 1950).

71 The complex dialectic of activity and passivity has been explicated with great sensitivity by Freud in his essay "Instincts and Their Vicissitudes," vol. 14 of *The Standard Edition of the Complete Psychological Works of Sigmund Freud,* (London: Hogarth, 1953-1973).

72 R. P. Taylor, ed., *The Computer in the School: Tutor, Tool, Tutee* (New York: Teachers College Press, 1980); P. Suppes, "Computer-Based Mathematics Instruction," *Bulletin of the International Study Group for Mathematical Learning* 3 (1965): 215-230; Kohl, "Should I Buy My Child a Computer?"; Davy, "Mindstorms in the Lamplight," (in this book).

73 R. Jastrow, "Toward an Intelligence Beyond Man's," *Time,* 20 February, 1978, 31-32.

74 Hence the frequent conflation of the children's actual mastery with their *sense of* mastery, a confusion made by S. Turkle in *The Second Self: Computers and the Human Spirit* (New York: Simon and Schuster, 1984), Papert in *Mindstorms,* Kohl in "Should I Buy My Child a Computer?" and other writers on electronic learning. The historical roots of this confusion are

traced in J. M. Broughton, "The Genetic Psychology of James Mark Baldwin," *American Psychologist* 36 (1981): 396-407; and its political implications are explored in J. M. Broughton and M. K. Zahaykevich, "Personality and Ideology in Ego Development," in *La Dialectique dans les Sciences Sociales,* ed. J. Gabel and V. Trinh van Thao (Paris: Anthropos, 1980).

75 R. P. Taylor, Introduction to *The Computer in the School,* p. 4 (second emphasis added).

76 Dreyfus, *What Computers Can't Do.*

77 Papert, *Mindstorms,* p. 18.

78 G. Simmel, "On the Concept and the Tragedy of Culture," in *The Conflict in Modern Culture and Other Essays* (New York: Teachers College Press, 1968).

79 W. E. Hocking, *Types of Philosophy* (New York: Scribner's, 1929).

80 Papert, *Mindstorms,* p. 4.

81 Horkheimer, *"The Concept of Man";* T. W. Adorno, "Sociology and Psychology," *New Left Review* 47 (1968) 90-115; M. Foucault, *Discipline and Punish: The Birth of the Prison* (New York: Vintage Books, 1979); C. Lasch, *The Minimal Self* (New York: Norton, 1984).

82 Papert, *Mindstorms,* p. 27 (emphasis in original).

83 Ibid.

84 Ibid., p. 9.

CONTRIBUTORS

STEPHEN ARONS, associate professor of legal studies at the University of Massachusetts at Amherst, is author of *Compelling Belief: The Culture of American Schooling*. He is former senior attorney at the Harvard Center on Law and Education, and writes frequently about issues of schooling and constitutional law.

RONALD H. BRADY is associate professor of philosophy at Ramapo College, Mahwah, New Jersey. His studies have focused on the relation between phenomenology and philosophy of science. He has published several articles on biological theory and is currently writing on biological teleology.

HARRIET K. CUFFARO is a member of the graduate faculty at Bank Street College of Education where she teaches courses, supervises teachers, and coordinates an intern program. As a curriculum specialist, she has contributed to the development of nonsexist and multicultural programs and materials. Her publications reflect her interest in issues of equity and young children's dramatic play and block building. She currently holds a John Dewey Senior Research Fellowship from the Center for Dewey Studies.

JOHN DAVY, O.B.E., M.A. (Cantab) is principal of Emerson College in Forest Row, Sussex, England. Formerly a zoologist, and then science editor for *The Observer* in London, he now has particular responsibility for the Foundation Year at Emerson College. This provides a general basis for various forms of training inspired by the work of Rudolf Steiner, and is a requirement for the Waldorf (Steiner-based) teacher training course at the college.

HUBERT L. DREYFUS is professor of philosophy at the University of California, Berkeley. He has published articles on phenomenology as well as a book on the limits of artificial intelligence, *What Computers Can't Do*.

STUART DREYFUS is professor of industrial engineering and operations research at the University of California, Berkeley, and is the author of three books on mathematical modeling for management.

JEFFREY KANE is assistant professor of education at Adelphi University where he teaches courses in educational philosophy. His principal interests have been in the philosophy of science and educational independence. He has written *Beyond Empiricism: Michael Polanyi Reconsidered* and a variety of essays and journal articles.

ROBERT L. LARSON is associate professor of administration and planning at the College of Education and Social Services, The University of Vermont. His research interests have focused on change processes in school improvement efforts with an emphasis on the socio-psychological dimensions of organizational innovation.

ANN LIEBERMAN is chairperson and professor in the Department of Curriculum and Teaching, associate director of the Horace Mann–Lincoln Institute, and executive secretary of the Metropolitan School Study Council at Teachers College, Columbia University. Her primary interest has been in educational change and school improvement. She has, for the last decade, attempted to bridge the gap between those studying how to improve schools and those working in them.

JOSEPH A. MENOSKY is a writer and radio producer living in Santa Monica, California. He has been the science editor at National Public Radio and is currently writing a column on technology for *Science 84* magazine.

DOUGLAS NOBLE has taught in alternative elementary, junior high, and adult education in Rochester, New York. A former programmer and computer instructor, he presently is seeking funding to work on the problem of education and the degradation of work.

ROBERT J. SARDELLO is director of studies at the Dallas Institute of Humanities and Culture. He has occupied the positions of dean of the graduate schools, director of the Institute of Philosophic Studies, and chairman of the psychology department at the University of Dallas. Dr. Sardello is the author of numerous articles on the phenomena of psychological experience and contemporary culture. He is a psychotherapist in private practice, and has been a guest professor at Sonoma State University, Seattle University, the University of New Mexico, and the Summer Institute in Archetypal Psychology at Notre Dame University.

BRIAN SIMPSON studied psychology and philosophy at Oxford University and went on to be personal skills training consultant and education methods adviser for IBM (UK). He is now an independent consultant, offering training and consultancy services in management and interpersonal skills, educational design, and instructor training and development. He may be contacted at 36 Milton Park, London 56 5QA, England (telephone 01-341 7201).

DAVID TYACK, professor of education at Stanford University, is co-author of *Managers of Virtue* (Basic Books, 1982) and *Public Schools in Hard Times* (Harvard University Press, 1984).

DONALD WARREN is professor and department chairman of education policy, planning, and administration at the University of Maryland. His research and publication focus on the history of federal education policy and the uses of history in policy analysis.

ARTHUR G. ZAJONC is assistant professor of physics at Amherst College. His areas of research include laser and atomic physics, and the history of science. He is particularly interested in the scientific work of Goethe.

ROBERT W. ZUBER, JR., received his doctorate in the field of religion and education from Teachers College, Columbia University. He has published several articles, two of which are to appear in *Religious Education* during 1985. Dr. Zuber does moral education with the Ethical Culture School of New York and is an instructor in the Peace Studies Program at Teachers College.

INDEX